PUTIN TAKES CRIMEA 2014

Grey-zone warfare opens the Russia-Ukraine conflict

MARK GALEOTTI

OSPREY PUBLISHING
Bloomsbury Publishing Plc
Kemp House, Chawley Park, Cumnor Hill, Oxford OX2 9PH, UK
29 Earlsfort Terrace, Dublin 2, Ireland
1385 Broadway, 5th Floor, New York, NY 10018, USA
Email: info@ospreypublishing.com
www.ospreypublishing.com

OSPREY is a trademark of Osprey Publishing Ltd

First published in Great Britain in 2023

© Osprey Publishing Ltd, 2023

A catalogue record for this book is available from the British Library.

ISBN: PB 9781472853844; eBook 9781472853875;
ePDF 9781472853851; XML 9781472853868
23 24 25 26 27   10 9 8 7 6 5 4 3 2 1

Battlescenes by Irene Cano Rodríguez
Cover art by Irene Cano Rodríguez
Maps by www.bounford.com
3D BEV by Alan Gilliland
Index by Zoe Ross
Typeset by PDQ Digital Media Solutions, Bungay, UK
Printed and bound in India by Replika Press Private Ltd.

Osprey Publishing supports the Woodland Trust, the UK's leading
woodland conservation charity.

To find out more about our authors and books visit www.ospreypublishing.
com. Here you will find extracts, author interviews, details of forthcoming
events and the option to sign up for our newsletter.

Author's note

Translating out of foreign alphabets always poses challenges. For Cyrillic,
I have chosen to transliterate names as they are pronounced, and have also
ignored the diacritical 'soft' and 'hard' signs found in the original. The only
exceptions are names that have acquired common forms in English – for
example, I use the spelling 'Gorbachev' rather than the phonetically correct
'Gorbachov'. There are also political minefields to be traversed. Ukrainian
words, names and places are transliterated Ukrainian-style, although Kiev is
used for the historical city, and Kyiv for today's Ukrainian capital. Territories
and cities largely occupied by Russian-speakers are rendered in their own
style. For names, the individuals' preferred forms are used.

Cover

As a force of Russian Naval Infantry 'little green men' accompanied by more
excitable local 'self-defence volunteers' move into the centre of Simferopol,
the lead soldier warns off a police officer who is incautiously blocking their
path. A second marine is keeping headquarters informed. Behind them is a
GAZ *Tigr* light utility vehicle, a versatile workhorse of the operation, here
mounting a 7.62mm Pecheneg machine gun. By this time, the Russians
were stretching the thin fiction of deniability to breaking point, and a
Mi-24 gunship flies low over the city, as much for the psychological effect
as because it may be needed to provide fire support.

Glossary of terms and acronyms used in this text

AD	Air Defence
APC	Armoured Personnel Carrier
ASSR	Autonomous Soviet Socialist Republic
AT	Antitank
BSF	Black Sea Fleet
BTG	Battalion Tactical Group
EU	European Union
FSB	Federal Security Service (Russian domestic security agency)
GOU	Main Operations Directorate of the (Russian) General Staff
GRU	Main Intelligence Directorate (Russian military intelligence, technically renamed GU in 2010)
IFV	Infantry Fighting Vehicle
KGB	Committee of State Security (Soviet intelligence and political police agency)
KSSO	Special Operations Forces Command (Russian)
LMV	Light Mobility Vehicle
MANPADS	Man-Portable Air Defence System
MLRS	Multiple-Launch Rocket System
MRAU	Massed Missile-Aviation Strike
MVS	Ukrainian Ministry of Internal Affairs
NTsUO	National Defence Management Centre (Russian)
OMON	Special Purpose Motorised Police
RPG	Rocket-Propelled Grenade [launcher]
SAM	Surface-to-Air Missile
SBU	Security Service of Ukraine
SVR	Foreign Intelligence Service (Russian)
VDV	Air Assault Troops (Russian paratroopers)
ZSU	Ukrainian Armed Forces (also sometimes rendered as VSU, from the Russian)

Order of battle abbreviations:

AA	Antiaircraft
Abn	Airborne
AD	Air Defence
Arty	Artillery
Bde	Brigade
Bn	Battalion
Co	Company
Div	Division
Indep	Independent
Inf	Infantry
Lt	Light
Mech	Mechanized
MR	Motor Rifle
Recon	Reconnaissance
Rgt	Regiment
Sub	Submarine
u/i	Unidentified

CONTENTS

INTRODUCTION 4
A history of conquest 4
After the Union 7
Euromaiden 8

ORIGINS 11
Political war 11
Copying a misunderstood West 14
New tools 16

THE PLAN 21
Preparations 23

THE OPERATION 27
A growing tension 29
The hidden hand 31
Preparations for conquest 33
Vremya Cha 35
Bottling up the peninsula 37
28 February 39
1 March and the 'Crimean Spring' 42
Taking the navy 45
Phoney war and real deaths 48
Taking the bases 50
Digging in 56

CONSOLIDATION 58

ANALYSIS 62
How special was this operation? 62
Crimea and the Donbas 63
The Kerch Strait Incident 65

CONCLUSION 69
Lessons learned – and misunderstood 69
The Crimean bastion 71
Crimea and the 2022 invasion 74

FURTHER READING 79

INDEX 80

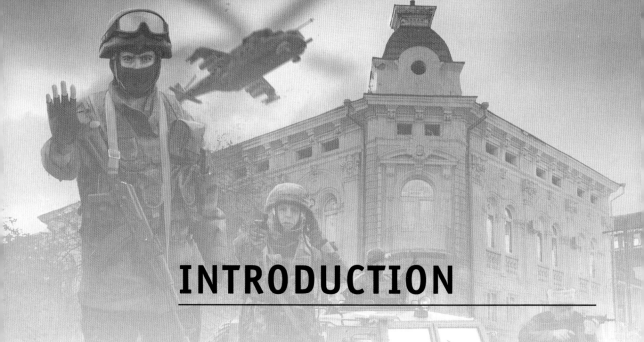

INTRODUCTION

Russia's annexation of the Crimea in 2014 was an almost bloodless conquest. It was, however, a crucial operation for our understanding of modern warfare, fought as much through propaganda, cyberattacks and subversion as force of arms, and features a fascinating – if often dysfunctional – series of characters and episodes, from Russian special forces and Ukrainian defectors, to gangsters sworn in as 'self-defence volunteers', and even naval confrontations. Whether known by the problematic term 'hybrid warfare' or the later 'grey zone warfare', terms which are dissected below, it is an example of a type of military confrontation increasingly to be found in the 21st century, where soldiers are introduced not at the beginning of the conflict but the end, after it has already all but been won through other, so-called 'non-kinetic' means.

Ironically, though, in the longer run, it also triggered the largest conventional land war in Europe since the Second World War. Although not what Moscow was planning when it took Crimea, that operation generated or encouraged an insurgency in Ukraine's south-eastern Donbas region, a toxic mix of civil war and undeclared Russian military intervention. And that, in turn, led to the fateful full-scale invasion of Ukraine in February 2022.

A history of conquest

Jutting out from the northern coast of the Black Sea, adjacent to the Sea of Azov, the 27,000 square km (10,000 square miles) of the Crimean Peninsula has been a trading crossroads and naval base for more than two millennia. In the fifth century BC, the Greeks established colonies on the coast of what became known as the Tauric Peninsula, after the Tauri who settled the north. Bithynians from Heraclea Pontica built the settlement of Chersonesos to the south-west of the territory, but over time, the south became consolidated into the Kingdom of the Cimmerian Bosporus. This was then seized by the Black Sea Kingdom of Pontus, whose centre of gravity was in northern Turkey, and then that became a Roman client state in 63 BC.

While for centuries the south of the Tauric Peninsula would be shaped by Greek culture, even if politically dominated by Rome and then Byzantium, its north would be subject to numerous invasions and influences, including the Kievan Rus' and then a changing cast of steppe nomads, including in due course the Mongols. Its value as a trading centre – the Black Sea was an intersection between Europe and the Middle East – also brought the Italians. The mercantile powers of Genoa and Venice established stations and took port cities, fighting campaigns against the Mongols and hiring out their mercenaries to competing Rus' princes. Indeed, while the indigenous Crimean Tatars called the peninsula Qirim, the modern name Crimea is the Italianized version.

As the Mongol Golden Horde began to decline, the Crimean Khanate emerged as its local successor, and in the 15th century this was in turn brought under the control of the Ottoman Empire. This was not only considered an affront by the rising power of Muscovy – especially as the Russian Orthodox Church traced its roots back to the baptism of Prince Vladimir of Kiev in Chersonesos in AD 988 – but also a practical threat. The Tatars would launch raids northwards to seize slaves, and so as part of its wider struggle against the Ottomans for regional hegemony, the rising Russian Empire annexed Crimea in 1783.

Given its strategic location, it later became a tempting target when the French and the British were looking for a way to take their war to Russia, leading to the ill-fated 1854–55 Crimean War. Although the great Russian

The peninsula has a long history of conquest and intrigue, but also as a place of trade, prosperity, leisure and beauty, as well as for a mix of nations and cultures. For example, the iconic Swallow's Nest, a folly on the coastline near Yalta, was built in the early 20th century for a Baltic German baron who had made a fortune with oil from Azerbaijan and hired a Russian architect to build something in Neo-Gothic style, as popularized by a Briton... (Photo by DeAgostini/Getty Images)

For reasons as much political as strategic, the port city of Sevastopol, shown in this 19th-century etching, became the target for the Franco–Russian invasion in 1854. After an 11-month siege, Sevastopol fell in September 1855. (Photo by Fine Art Images/Heritage Images/Getty Images)

The Black Sea Fleet has long been a crucial element of Russian power projection. Here, the battleships *Rostislav, Ioann Zlatoust* and *Yevstafi* get under steam at Sevastopol in 1910. The latter two were the most modern ships in the Black Sea Fleet at the start of the First World War, which all three survived, only to end up in Allied hands when they intervened during the Russian Civil War, handed to the anti-Bolshevik White forces and then abandoned, unseaworthy, when the Whites evacuated Crimea in 1920. (Photo by Pictures From History/Universal Images Group via Getty Images)

naval base of Sevastopol fell after an 11-month siege, the war was really decided in the Baltic and White Seas, and once it became clear that she risked an economic blockade, Russia sued for peace.[1]

Nonetheless, Crimea remained in Russian hands. In the chaos of the collapse of tsarism, the Bolshevik Revolution and the 1918–22 Russian Civil War, a dozen different administrations and regimes claimed it, and Crimea saw the last stand of the White Russian anti-revolutionary forces of General Pyotr Wrangel in 1920, the survivors of which fled by sea to Istanbul. Crimea, or technically the Crimean Autonomous Soviet Socialist Republic (ASSR), crucially became part of not the Ukrainian but the Russian Soviet Federative Socialist Republic (RSFSR).

Briefly occupied by the Germans from 1942–43 during the Second World War, after it had been retaken by the Soviets, it witnessed the mass deportation of the 200,000-strong Crimean Tatar population in 1944, half dying on the way. Stalin claimed that this was because they had collaborated with the Germans – although this was true only of a small minority – but it rather represented an act of ethnic cleansing, intended so that Russian colonists could take their place. The Tatars were resettled in Siberia and Central Asia, and while technically freed from Stalin's decree in 1967, in practice they were only allowed to return in 1991.

After the war, the Crimean ASSR became simply the Crimean Oblast (Region) of the RSFSR, but in 1954, to mark the 300th anniversary of the 1654 Pereyaslav Agreement whereby Ukrainian Cossacks swore allegiance to the tsar, it was transferred to the Ukrainian Soviet Socialist Republic. At the time, this seemed an essentially empty gesture, albeit one that reflected the degree to which Crimea depended on water and electricity from the neighbouring Ukrainian Kherson region, to which it is connected by the Perekop Isthmus. After all, it was still part of the same Soviet Union. However, this would prove a fateful decision in 1991, when that union fell apart.

1   *See* Mungo Melvin, *Sevastopol's Wars* (Osprey, 2017).

After the Union

Legally, Crimea was Ukraine's, but it was clear that it felt different and believed it had been neglected by Kyiv. In a referendum in 1990, while almost all Ukrainians had voted for independence from the USSR, only 56 per cent did so in Crimea. After all, the majority of its 2.4 million population considered themselves to be Russian, ethnically, culturally and linguistically, especially as many retired officers from the Black Sea Fleet (BSF), headquartered in Sevastopol, had chosen to settle there with their families.

Indeed the BSF itself was a serious bone of contention. The understanding was that Soviet non-nuclear military forces and assets would devolve to whichever new state controlled the territory on which they were based, and so in 1993, when Kyiv formally established the Ukrainian Navy, this was essentially the BSF. However, the BSF comprised some 80,000 servicemen, including Naval Infantry (marine) units, 69 major warships including the aircraft carrier *Baku* (soon renamed the *Admiral Gorshkov*), 29 submarines and fully 235 fixed and rotary-wing aircraft. Moscow was not willing to give up such a powerful asset as well as Russia's claims to being a Black Sea naval power, and disputes between pro-Kyiv and pro-Moscow elements of the fleet quickly erupted. At the end of 1991, Ukrainian President Leonid Kravchuk ordered all military units in Ukraine to pledge allegiance to the new state by 20 January 1992: the great majority of the BSF simply ignored him.

In January 1992, Russia's parliament, the Supreme Soviet, questioned the constitutionality of that 1954 decision, while grass-roots protests began in Crimea itself against being part of the new Ukrainian state. In April, in response to Kyiv's attempts to assert its control over the entire BSF and appoint Admiral Borys Kozhyn in command, Russian President Boris Yeltsin issued a decree stating that the fleet was Russia's.

Appreciating the dangers in this 'battle of decrees', both sides agreed to suspend further action while they held talks to resolve the crisis. Initially, a rather clumsy compromise saw the BSF become a joint force under bilateral command, although it was understood that Moscow would still appoint the overall commander. This was just an interim measure, though, and in May 1997, after long and difficult negotiations against a backdrop of continuing clashes between pro-Kyiv and pro-Moscow sailors, an agreement was signed on the partition of the fleet.

More than three-quarters of the BSF that had been based in Crimea went to Russia, in return for which Moscow paid

In many ways, the roots of the 2014 annexation lay just as much in the clumsy and conflicted division of the Black Sea Fleet as in the earlier transfer of the peninsula from Russia to Ukraine. Most Russians never accepted this and felt that, as the makeshift banner behind the two 'little green men' says, 'Crimea is Russia'. These Russian special forces are securing the Crimean parliament in Simferopol on 1 March 2014. (Photo by Sean Gallup/Getty Images)

Ukraine had long considered the possibility of a Russian invasion. Here, a Ukrainian officer examines a huge map during military exercises in 2008, amidst growing tensions with Russia. Nonetheless, many in government refused to take this seriously, and in any case the state was in disarray following the downfall of Yanukovych's government. (SERGEI SUPINSKY/AFP via Getty Images)

Kyiv compensation to the tune of $526 million. In addition, the Russians would continue to maintain their naval bases on the peninsula, leased from Ukraine for an additional $97 million a year, for an initial period of 20 years that was subsequently extended until 2042. Beyond the BSF's ships, Russia would limit its presence in Crimea to 25,000 troops, 24 artillery systems, 132 armoured vehicles and 22 aircraft. Furthermore, the Ukrainian Navy was also headquartered in Crimea, at Sevastopol – just streets from the Russian BSF's base.

Officially, Moscow also agreed to 'respect the sovereignty of Ukraine, honour its legislation and avoid interfering in Ukraine's internal affairs'. Indeed, in 2008, Putin had hit out at any thought that Moscow had designs on the peninsula, saying, 'Crimea is not a contentious territory… Russia has long ago recognized the borders of today's Ukraine…. I consider the idea that Russia would have such aims to be a provocation.'

In practice, tensions would surface periodically. In 2009, for example, Ukrainian President Viktor Yushchenko, no friend of Moscow's, threatened that the lease would not be extended and that the BSF would have to leave by 2017 – knowing that Russia lacked adequate alternative facilities on the Black Sea. This was, however, more hardball negotiation than a real likelihood. Nonetheless, it was to prove a dangerous bargaining tactic in that it left Moscow with the uneasy sense that its foothold in Crimea might be more precarious than it would like, something that would prove significant in 2014.

Euromaidan

Ukraine's turbulent politics had seen Kyiv charting an erratic course between Moscow and the West, tied to Russia by history, economic pragmatism and the sentiment of many within the disproportionately Russian-speaking east of the country, yet eager for the potential investment, freedoms and support of Europe. In 2013, this reached a climax when President Viktor Yanukovych first agreed to sign an Association Agreement with the European Union (EU), then reversed his position under Russian pressure. To Vladimir Putin, who regarded Ukraine not so much as a real state but a part of Russia's sphere of influence and historical birth right, this was not simply an insult; it reflected covert Western attempts to undermine Moscow's status.

A closer relationship with the EU was popular in the country, though, and Yanukovych's last-minute decision triggered a wave of protests and civil unrest which focused on Maidan Nezalezhnosti (Independence Square) in central Kyiv. Yanukovych managed to worsen the situation, threatening then using force against the protesters, both by police and the thugs who became known as *titushki*, hooligans who tried to provoke incidents and beat up protesters. This all proved extremely counterproductive. As a Russian riot police officer who had been attached to the Ukrainian Ministry of Internal Affairs put it to the author, the regime applied 'enough violence to radicalise, not enough to win'.

The governments new tougher line failed to stem the protest movement, and on 23 February 2014 it became known that Yanukovych had fled to asylum in Russia. The 'Euromaidan' rising, also known as the Revolution of Dignity, cost the lives of 108 protesters and 13 members of the security forces, but more importantly marked a decisive break in Ukraine's domestic and foreign affairs, with the EU Association Agreement signed in March. An interim government under new Prime Minister Arseny Yatsenyuk took power before early presidential elections could be held in May, which saw 'Chocolate King' billionaire Petro Poroshenko win in the first round.

Putin was furious and denounced the revolution as an illegal seizure of power, and there were also those within Ukraine who were uncomfortable with the new order, especially Russian-speaking citizens who feared they faced discrimination. More to the point, Ukraine's state apparatus had virtually collapsed. The military chain of command in many cases simply evaporated, especially because many senior officers either defected to the Russians or were arrested, dismissed or suspended for suspected pro-Moscow sympathies. As protests and violent risings spread in the predominantly Russian-speaking Donbas region in the south-east, the regular police and military would prove simply unable adequately to respond. Rebel militias increasingly would be confronted by loyalist ones, albeit units which often did not heed Kyiv's orders. This helps explain why, in March, Kyiv established a National Guard, in part precisely to plug the gap and provide a structure to try to incorporate these Volunteer Battalions. Furthermore,

An anti-government protester throws a Molotov cocktail during clashes with police on Hrushevskoho Street near Dynamo stadium in Kyiv on 25 January 2014. After two months of essentially peaceful anti-government protests, the government's efforts to disperse the protests actually radicalized it, leading to violent clashes through the centre of the city. (Photo by Brendan Hoffman/ Getty Images)

Berkut riot police in their distinctive blue tiger-striped urban camouflage fire rubber bullets towards anti-government protesters on Kyiv's Independence Square on 19 February 2014. The Berkut officers became symbolic of the Yanukovych regime's efforts to suppress the protests by violent means. (Photo by Brendan Hoffman/Getty Images)

the infamous Berkut riot police was disbanded because of their violent repression of protesters (*see* box), which in practice meant most defected to the Russians or joined anti-government insurgents in the south-eastern Donbas region.

The immediate issue was Crimea, though. On 22 February, Putin convened an all-night meeting with a small circle of his security chiefs and closest advisers. The task at hand was how to get Yanukovych out of Russia safely – today's Russian rulers, like the Soviet KGB in which so many of them served, understand how important it is to get 'their people' back. As the meeting broke up in the early hours, though, Putin turned to his underlings and added that 'we must start working on returning Crimea to Russia'.

BERKUT: YANUKOVYCH'S STORMTROOPERS

Berkut (Golden Eagle) was a specialized armed unit within the Ministry of Internal Affairs (MVS), established in 1992 on the basis of the Ukrainian element of the former Soviet OMON riot police. Their roles ranged from public order missions to providing armed support for raids on organized crime hangouts, but they acquired an unsavoury reputation for their thuggish ways and their willingness to be used by the government of the day to harass opponents and suppress the opposition. Each Ukrainian region or city had its own Berkut unit, with strengths ranging from a 50-man company to a full regiment of 600. As of 2013, there were two regiments, six battalions, and 19 companies, with a total strength of almost 3,500. They typically wore blue tiger-striped urban camouflage and maroon berets or camouflage caps, and were equipped with 9mm PM Makarov or Fort-12 pistols, 7.62mm AKM assault rifles, Fort-500 shotguns and 7.62mm SVD Dragunov sniper rifles, with heavier support weapons available when necessary. Berkut played a violent role in attempting to suppress the 'Revolution of Dignity' and so was formally dissolved in 2014, many of its roles being taken over in due course by the new National Guard. A majority of its members, though, defected to Russia or Crimea, joining militants in the Donbas or being enrolled into Russia's OMON.

ORIGINS

The roots of the Crimean annexation may be in history and geopolitics, but the origins of the way Moscow carried it out are to be found in its evolving understanding of warfighting in the twenty-first century. The elements – misdirection, subversion, the use of covert and deniable forces and lightning special forces operations – were all familiar, but the way they were used reflected how Russian thinking about war had been informed by a chain of learning experiences, from earlier political operations, through the Soviet war in Afghanistan, to the wars in Chechnya and the 2008 invasion of Georgia. Ironically, these drew on much older operational concepts as well as, to be blunt, a serious misunderstanding of Western interventions in Iraq, Kosovo and Libya and beyond.

Political war

The Russians are, after all, heirs to a long tradition of military thinking, predating even the Soviet era, that regards 'war' in more holistic terms than the West, not recognising sharp boundaries between warfighting, subversion, espionage and influence operations. Through its own imperial wars, tsarist Russia had long embraced a wide and wily range of means. They recruited former enemies such as the Cossacks, and placed a heavy emphasis on assassination, subversion and disinformation. The Soviets, who saw everything in political terms, were even more willing to use any means at their disposal to achieve their goals. They tested out their ideas both in colonial wars such as the reconquest of Central Asia during the Russian Civil War with the brutal pacification of the *basmachestvo* national rebellions and their efforts to extend their own influence in Europe. In the former conflict, for example, they even employed early special forces, the Units of Special Designation, as 'pseudo-gangs', pretending to be rebels either to spring ambushes or mount provocations and false flag operations to tarnish their enemies' reputations. In the latter, they foreshadowed the way officially denied forces with no evident

Cossacks have, since tsarist times, been used as instruments of the state, but in the modern era they have played a particular role as deniable tools of Kremlin foreign policy. Here, two Cossacks in the traditional papakha fur hats of Kuban Cossacks, guard a lobby in the regional administration headquarters in Donetsk in July 2014, in the early stages of the Donbas conflict, before Moscow was yet willing to become openly involved. (MAXV VETROV/ AFP via Getty Images)

insignia could work with local allies in an attempted take-over of Estonia in 1924 (*see* box).

In 1929, the Bolsheviks had staged an abortive invasion of Afghanistan in the midst of a rebellion, but they withdrew within two months. Fifty years later, though, when the Soviets stumbled incautiously into Afghanistan (1979–88), they again fought not just a conventional counter-insurgency against the *mujahideen* rebels but also an often-sophisticated political operation. Tribal warlords were co-opted or set against each other, disinformation mobilized both in the country and also to try to undermine

THE ESTONIAN PUTSCH, 1924

The leadership of the young Bolshevik state believed that the Soviet Union was just the first socialist state – and that it was both necessary for its survival and also a moral duty to spread the credo, by any means necessary. The local Communist Party in Estonia was keen for Moscow's assistance to seize power, and was preparing a coup with the support of Razvedupr, Soviet military intelligence (the precursor to the modern GRU). On 1 December 1924, almost 300 Communists, many trained in the USSR, supported by Soviet agents, tried to seize key government and military installations around Tallinn, the capital. The expectation was that they would spontaneously be joined by downtrodden workers and soldiers, but more to the point that they could declare a revolutionary government which could 'invite' fraternal 'assistance' from the USSR. Soviet naval forces were already at sea, and ground forces

mobilized on the pretext of a training exercise near the border. Aircraft were also on standby, as one of the main objectives was Tallinn airfield, which would allow the quick deployment of an advance guard of Soviet troops. The revolutionaries had some limited successes at first, but the government moved quickly to declare a state of emergency, the proletariat proved markedly unwilling to rise, and the security forces began to reassert control, including retaking the airfield. There is no question but that the Red Army could have simply invaded Estonia, had it chosen. However, the Soviet Union, riven by political rivalries after Lenin's recent death and still an international pariah, was not yet willing to engage in an openly imperial venture. Moscow backed down. It pulled its covert operators from Estonia when it could, and disavowed any role in the attempted coup.

Russia's use of deniable local allies and proxies was especially evident in Crimea. Here, for example, members of so-called 'people's militia' or 'local self-defence units' gather outside the Crimean regional parliament building while parliamentarians are voting on a proposed referendum on Crimean autonomy. Their purpose was as much to intimidate the deputies as protest the building, and in due course the clubs they are holding would be replaced with guns that had already been stockpiled in the peninsula. (Photo by Sean Gallup/Getty Images)

Western involvement, and provocations and 'false flag' operations were launched to discredit and divide the rebels.[2]

After the end of the USSR, Russian military thinkers were also freer to draw on writers who had previously been considered politically incorrect. One such was Yevgeny Messner, a tsarist officer who had fought against the Bolsheviks during the Russian Civil War before fleeing to Belgrade. In his *Myatezh: imya tretyey vsemirnoy* ('Subversion: the name of the Third World War', 1960), he predicted that:

> Future war will not be fought on the front lines, but throughout the entire territories of both opponents, because behind the front lines, political, social, and economic fronts will appear; they will fight not on a two-dimensional plane, as in olden days, not in a three dimensional space, as has been the case since the birth of military aviation, but in a four-dimensional space, where the psyche of the combatant nations will serve as the fourth dimension.

This notion that 'the psyche of combatant nations' is a specific domain of battle, while not new in principle – all wars are really struggles of will – became especially important in a Russia that would be trying to assert its status as a great power when its economic, political and military resources were only a fraction of the USSR's. Increasingly, especially after Vladimir Putin's ascension to the presidency in 2000, Russia would find itself adopting tactics that, if anything, were closest to what veteran scholar-diplomat George Kennan, architect of American strategy in the early Cold War, called 'political warfare':

2   *See* Gregory Fremont-Barnes, *The Soviet–Afghan War 1979–89*, Essential Histories series (Osprey, 2012).

… the employment of all the means at a nation's command, short of war, to achieve its national objectives. Such operations are both overt and covert. They range from such overt actions as political alliances, economic measures (as ERP—the Marshall Plan), and 'white' propaganda to such covert operations as clandestine support of 'friendly' foreign elements, 'black' psychological warfare and even encouragement of underground resistance in hostile states.

Copying a misunderstood West

It was not just that the Russians had to rely more on subversion and misdirection because they knew they were trying to punch above their weight (although that was true). It was also precisely because they – or at least Vladimir Putin and the coterie of KGB veterans in his inner circle – assumed that this was how the West was operating. In an age of popular protests, they interpreted such events as the 'Colour Revolutions' in neighbouring post-Soviet states (including Georgia's 2003 Rose Revolution, Ukraine's 2004 Orange Revolution and Kyrgyzstan's 2005 Tulip Revolution) and the 'Arab Spring' risings in the early 2010s, not as organic protests against often corrupt and authoritarian regimes, but as examples of Western-fomented subversion. As one Russian thinktanker close to the Kremlin put it to the author, 'We see the hand of the CIA in this mischief.' The fact that many of the regimes facing such revolutions were allies of Moscow, or at least customers for its weapons, was considered 'proof' enough.

In 2013, Russian Chief of the General Staff General Valery Gerasimov made a pretty routine speech to the Academy of Military Sciences that was subsequently reprinted in the distinctly niche *Military-Industrial Courier*. At

As part of its counter to what it believed was a US-led campaign of subversion in Russia's self-proclaimed sphere of influence, Moscow would recruit whatever local allies it could. Here, a former Berkut special police officer who has defected to the forces of the 'Lugansk People's Republic' stands guard at a checkpoint near Schastya. Note the under-barrel 40mm grenade launcher on his AKMS rifle. (ANATOLII BOIKO/AFP via Getty Images)

Alexander 'Surgeon' Zaldostanov, leader of the Night Wolves motorcycle group, attends a rally of pro-Russian activists in Simferopol on 28 February. To be blunt, the Night Wolves were there more for show than because they played a particularly significant role in the overall take-over of the peninsula, but they made the most of the opportunity to play the role of tough champions of the Russian cause. (Genya SAVILOV/AFP via Getty Images)

the time, the article, with the far-from-snappy title 'The Value of Science is in the Foresight: new challenges demand rethinking the forms and methods of carrying out combat operations', attracted little attention. In light of the Crimean operation, though, it began to be taken as identifying a whole new Russian way of war, a veritable 'Gerasimov Doctrine' (*see* box). The irony was that Gerasimov was actually talking about what he thought was the new *Western* way of war when he wrote:

> In the 21st century, we have seen a tendency toward a blurring of the lines between the states of war and peace. Wars are no longer declared and, having begun, proceed according to an unfamiliar template… [whereby] a perfectly thriving state can, in a matter of months and even days, be transformed into an arena of fierce armed conflict, become a victim of foreign intervention, and sink into a web of chaos, humanitarian catastrophe, and civil war…

THE 'GERASIMOV DOCTRINE' THAT WASN'T

Confession is meant to be good for the soul, but the author must admit with all due guilt that he was responsible for originally – if unintentionally – publicizing the term the 'Gerasimov Doctrine'. It was intended simply as a cute throwaway title for a post on my *In Moscow's Shadows* blog, evoking the title of thick paperback thrillers of the sort that especially populates airport bookshops. It was not meant to suggest that it was a 'doctrine' – the term has a very specific meaning in Russian military writing – or even that it was Gerasimov's, given that the original speech was likely drafted for him by his staff. Nonetheless, the title gained more traction than the actual discussion that followed, despite everything I could do. The reason for dwelling on this is to underline the degree to which uncertainty about the shape of future conflict means that there is a dangerously eager market for new buzzwords and generally the notion that somehow tomorrow's wars will be radically different from today's, when even in an age of drones, lasers and the internet of things, the fundamentals are still very much the same.

THE NIGHT WOLVES

The Night Wolves (*Nochnye Volki*) emerged in the 1980s Soviet Union, originally as a rebellious counter-culture group. Then, it stood for rock music, big motorcycles and overt rule breaking as a direct challenge to the staid and conservative official values of the Communist Party. Officially registered in 1989, in the 1990s it expanded across Russia and, reflecting the anarchy and often violence of the country's transition to capitalism, also became a commercial empire (with the Wolf Wear clothing brand and Wolf Engineering motorcycle custom shop, for example) and, it was widely alleged, a criminal one, too. In this respect, it very much followed in the path of the Hells Angels and similar Western outlaw motorcycle gangs. However, under Putin it increasingly became co-opted as an informal arm of the state. Putin used his relationship with the Night Wolves to shore up his macho credentials, even riding with them on a Harley-Davidson trike. More importantly, its members, whom Putin described as 'such courageous, tough guys', began to be used both to encourage muscular nationalism among Russian youth and spread Russian influence abroad, through their growing network of overseas affiliates. By 2013, they were receiving substantial sums from the Kremlin, ostensibly to cover their 'patriotic shows' and youth outreach work. However, this also seems to have bought their services for a range of overt and covert activities in support of Putin's policies. They provided volunteers in Crimea (at least 11 members were awarded the campaign medal 'For the Return of Crimea') and then the Donbas, tried to stage high-profile rides in Poland, Germany and elsewhere to publicize Russian propaganda, and were accused of trying to stir up inter-ethnic tensions in the Balkans. As a result, the organization has been barred from entry or sanctioned by many Western governments, including the United States. Nonetheless, it has an estimated global membership of 30,000–40,000, and in light of the worsening relations between Russia and the West following the 2022 invasion of Ukraine, has been described by one British intelligence official as 'a likely fifth column, outsourced intelligence-gathering asset, and all-round potential security worry'.

> The role of nonmilitary means of achieving political and strategic goals has grown, and, in many cases, they have exceeded the power of force of weapons in their effectiveness... All this is supplemented by military means of a concealed character, including carrying out actions of informational conflict and the actions of special-operations forces. The open use of forces – often under the guise of peacekeeping and crisis regulation – is resorted to only at a certain stage, primarily for the achievement of final success in the conflict.

So this was the threat the Kremlin was demanding that the military prepare to repel. Nonetheless, as the subsequent invasion of Ukraine in 2022 demonstrated, Russia had by no means abandoned full-scale mechanized warfare for a new 'doctrine' of indirect and deniable operations. Rather, it began to increase the attention it devoted to finding ways whereby new and old instruments of political war, from disinformation to mercenaries, could be used to support conventional military operations.

New tools

In the subsequent conflict in the Donbas, for example, the Russians would use mercenary organizations as deniable proxies, most notorious the Wagner Group Private Military Company (*Gruppa Vagner ChVK*). This would go on to operate in Syria, Libya, Venezuela and elsewhere in Africa before being mobilized for the 2022 invasion of Ukraine. In Crimea, though, they used more ad hoc proxy forces, including local gangsters, veterans of the Soviet war in Afghanistan, and even members of the Night Wolves motorcycle club (*see* box). Together, as will be discussed below, such bodies provided Moscow with muscle when needed. They were by no means as effective and professional as the so-called 'polite people' of the special forces, but they were deniable, expendable and helped generate the appearance that what was going on was a local rising, not a foreign invasion.

As already mentioned, for example, the new Ukrainian government has disbanded the Berkut special police units for their violent and sometimes lethal suppression of protesters during the revolution, leading many to turn against Kyiv. Crimea became a magnet, drawing those looking for both a cause and sanctuary, and Moscow gladly co-opted them. In particular, they were used to seal off the Perekop Isthmus that connected the peninsula to the mainland. Only 8km (5 miles) wide, Perekop is a strategic bottleneck for road and rail routes into Crimea, which Moscow needed to control. However, the early sight of Russian troops, whether acknowledged or not, nose to nose with Ukrainians on the isthmus would have quickly dispelled any hopes of deniability and risked triggering a direct clash sooner than they would have wanted. Thus, Moscow needed someone else to do the job instead of its own 'little green men'.

To this end, the Berkut unit from Sevastopol, which had just returned from Kyiv – a desperate Yanukovych had summoned everyone he thought might still be loyal – was deployed on the night of 26–27 February, on the ostensible orders of the so-called 'People's Mayor of Sevastopol' Aleksey Chaly. They established checkpoints on the three main roads into Crimea, the Kalanchak–Armyansk, Chaplynka–Armyansk and Chongar–Dzhankoy highways. They began checking vehicles going in and out of the peninsula, but mainly acted as both a symbol of secession and also a tripwire, ready to alert the Russians if any Ukrainian troops tried to force their way across the Perekop.

Beyond that, the Russians make particular use of 'information warfare', which in their especially broad definition means everything from disinformation to direct hacking of enemy critical infrastructure. Sometimes these cyberattacks are carried out by government agencies, notably the Federal Security Service (FSB), Foreign Intelligence Service (SVR) and military intelligence (the GRU, the Main Intelligence Directorate of the General Staff[3]), each of which had its own strengths and priorities.

---

3   Technically, this was known simply as the GU, the Main Directorate, from 2010, but universally it was and still is known by its older acronym.

BERKUT ROADBLOCK

Having been disbanded by the new government in Kyiv, perhaps it is no wonder that the Berkut riot police threw in their lot with the Crimeans – and, by extension, Moscow. On the night of 26–27 February, they set up roadblocks around Sevastopol and on the main highways into Crimea along the Perekop Isthmus. Here, early on the morning of the 27th, Berkutovtsy are controlling traffic along the T2202 road from Chaplynka in Kherson region to the Crimean town of Armyansk. The officer in the foreground is in the distinctive blue urban camouflage Berkut inherited from the Soviet OMON riot police and is cradling a Ukrainian-made Fort-500M shotgun.

In the background are two of his colleagues. One is searching an unfortunate delivery driver, who is from Kharkiv, if his FC Metalist Kharkiv football top is any indication. The other is standing guard. He is is wearing the maroon beret of the MVS Interior Troops and is carrying the folding stock 7.62mm AKMS-47 that was their standard rifle.

A mix of regular and proxy forces, typical of many 'grey zone' operations. A Russian BTR-80, part of a unit which relieved the previous Berkut force there, is parked behind sandbag defences at a checkpoint on the Armyansk road. Behind and to its right is an encampment of Cossack volunteers. (ALEXEY KRAVTSOV/AFP via Getty Images)

GRU's Unit 74455, for example, better known as Sandworm, Voodoo Bear and Iron Viking, is believed to have been responsible for sophisticated operations against Ukraine in 2015 and 2017, among other incidents. At other times, they were outsourced to criminal hackers or even, for want of a better expression, 'crowdsourced'. In these cases, such as a massive campaign against Estonia in 2007 and another against Georgia during the 2008 war, the government simply encouraged Russian hackers to launch attacks on the designated target, providing the online tools to allow even relatively inexperienced 'patriotic hackers' to play their role.

The term 'hybrid war' was first invoked in the West to explain Russia's use of both 'kinetic' military and non-military means in war, even though the term had originally been used for how non-state forces battled states, with the classic case being that of the Lebanese Hezbollah militant party's struggle with Israel. It found itself being used for an often-counterproductively wide range of situations, including ones in which Russia used no force at all and, frankly, began to lose what utility it had. As Latvian scholar Jānis Bērziņš has sharply noted, 'The word hybrid is catchy, since it may represent a mix of anything.'

Since then, there has been a parade of new terms – asymmetric war, sub-threshold operations, non-linear warfare – but as of writing, the favoured term appears to be 'grey zone warfare', operations somewhere in that hazy conceptual no-man's land between peace and full warfare. Certainly that is a space the Russians have eagerly and often effectively embraced, and the Crimean operation was an excellent example in which special forces, gangsters, political opportunists, hackers, disinformation and subversion came together in an effective unified campaign.

CYBERATTACKS AND CRIMEA

There was also an online dimension to the seizure of Crimea. The Russians quickly took over the peninsula's internet exchange and telecommunications centres, cutting the connection with the mainland and instead routing signals through a hurriedly laid new submarine cable into Russia. However, the real focus of Russian cyber operations was to contribute to the chaos and uncertainty in Kyiv. Government websites were shut down or defaced, with the National Security and Defence Council being a particular target; officials' and parliamentarians' mobile phones were jammed or hacked; a sophisticated programme known as Snake or Ouroboros, which had long been implanted into Ukrainian government systems, was activated, allowing its users to funnel out information and implant new malware (malicious software) at will. None of these attacks were decisive in their own right, but they undoubtedly contributed to the confusion which gave the Russians the time to complete their military fait accompli.

THE PLAN

The General Staff's Main Operations Directorate (GOU) had had contingency plans for taking Crimea that dated back to the 1990s, possibly even from 1992 and the 'battle of decrees'. It is, after all, its job to consider any such possibilities. There is no evidence that this reflected any serious intent to seize the peninsula at that time, nor that this progressed beyond an outline concept, and certainly not to a detailed operational plan. Indeed, according to one account, the cases containing this outline plan were almost lost when the GOU temporarily moved offices in 2008, the numerical codes being confused so that it was for a while misfiled as a contingency for an attack on Iran!

Nonetheless, by 18 February, when Yanukovych effectively introduced a state of emergency in Ukraine, those plans were already being revisited, and Russian forces in Crimea and some intervention units such as the 45th Independent Guards Special Designation Regiment of the Air Assault Troops (VDV) were being brought to full readiness. At this stage, it may simply

Pro-Russian supporters wave flags as they welcome the missile cruiser *Moskva* as it enters Sevastopol Bay in August 2008, after its participation in Russia's military operation in Georgia. Shortly thereafter, Kyiv began threatening not to extend the lease on Russian facilities in Crimea. The *Moskva* was the Black Sea Fleet flagship until it was destroyed by Ukrainian Neptune anti-shipping missiles in 2022. (Photo by VASILY BATANOV/AFP via Getty Images)

Ukrainian Border Guards with their trademark green berets – a holdover from Soviet times – coming on duty at the checkpoint of Kuchurgany, on the border with the unrecognized Russian dependency of the Pridnestrovian Moldavian Republic, or Transnistria. The annexation would ensure that such other territories with sizeable ethnic Russian or pro-Russian populations became considered potential targets for the 'next Crimea'. (ALEXEY KRAVTSOV/AFP via Getty Images)

again have been prudent contingency work by the GOU, but by the time Putin made his comment about 'working on returning Crimea to Russia' at 7am on the morning of 23 February, at least a preliminary political decision had already been made. That seems likely to have been on 20 February, even before the Yanukovych regime had fallen. After all, the commemorative campaign medal 'For the Return of Crimea', with its distinctive ribbon

THE MAIN OPERATIONS DIRECTORATE

While formally only one element of the sprawling General Staff apparatus – that includes two other Main Directorates, five Directorates, and seven other services, departments and centres – the Main Operations Directorate (GOU: *Glavnoye Operativnoye Upravleniye*) is undoubtedly the largest and most important, and its head is usually also a First Deputy Chief of the General Staff. It occupies about a tenth of the Defence Ministry's sprawling building on Frunze Embankment (Frunzenskaya Naberezhnaya, 22/2, Moscow, 119160), and has around a thousand staff (typically known as 'operators'), disproportionately drawn from the ground forces. Although it officially dates its history back to the foundation of the Quartermaster-General's Office in 1702, the GOU has its immediate roots in the 1st (Operations) Directorate of the General Staff, established in 1939 in response to the imminence of war. It evolved in the course of the 'Great Patriotic War' and became

the Main Operations Directorate in 1946. It became both the main planning and operational command element of the Soviet military, especially evolving under the pressure of managing the ten-year war in Afghanistan, 1979–88, and would maintain this role in post-Soviet Russia, despite occasional political tensions between the GOU head of the day and defence ministers who may have distrusted its power. It was the GOU that had drawn up the broad concept for seizing Crimea in the 1990s, and which was charged with hurriedly turning it into a detailed operational plan when Putin made his decision. Fortunately for them, the GOU's planning staff were used to anticipating the vagaries of their political superiors, and had therefore already begun carrying out preliminary work fleshing out the concept since early January, when the future of the Yanukovych regime was already looking doubtful.

mixing the Russian tricolour with the black and orange of the St George's ribbon, gives the dates of the operation as 20 February to 18 March. This seems to have been an accidental admission of the real time frame.

Who made the decision? Clearly Putin was the ultimate decider, but the people with whom he had his final discussions over whether to act appear to have been Nikolai Patrushev, the ultra-hawkish Secretary of the Security Council and in effect his national security adviser; Alexander Bortnikov, Director of the FSB; Sergei Ivanov, the head of the Presidential Administration; and Sergei Shoigu, Defence Minister. All but Shoigu were veterans of the Soviet KGB, and tellingly he appears to have been the only one of them who seems to have had his doubts. Persistent, if unconfirmed reports suggest he was concerned about the long-term consequences but was also wise enough to know that it was dangerous to stand against Putin when he had his mind set on something, especially when he was flanked by the other security chiefs. Ultimately, he simply declared that he would obey his orders. Figures such as Foreign Minister Sergei Lavrov who might have counselled against the move were not even invited to the discussions.

Preparations

Through 20 February, the planning cell within the GOU which had been working on an operational plan for the past couple of days began to firm up the details, while cutting orders for the various units which would be involved. One Russian officer who had been on the periphery of this effort described it as 'total creative chaos, all hands on deck as a whole operation was hammered out in something like 24 hours. It should have been a disaster, but these people knew what they were doing, and it just came together'. More to the point, a joint working group was set up to bring together the defence planners, GRU and the FSB. The GRU had long been working on penetrating the Ukrainian forces in Crimea, and would play a crucial role in facilitating a series of defections that would both ease the Russians' path and also support their narrative that this was a 'liberation' rather than an invasion. Meanwhile, the FSB had extensive networks of contacts and agents in Crimea, and would be busy ensuring a smooth handover of power as well as mobilizing local proxies, including gangsters, as both support for the regular military and a smokescreen.

By the end of 21 February, preparations moved from discussion to mobilization. Several elite intervention units began to be mobilized, under the cover of a wider series of military exercises that would at the same time worry and distract Kyiv. On the peninsula itself, BSF bases quietly

Barring the camouflage pattern of the uniform, there was relatively little to distinguish Ukrainian from Russian soldiers in 2014, both still heavily shaped by their Soviet ancestry. This Ukrainian soldier guarding the Belbek airbase carries the same AKM-74 rifle used by most of his Russian counterparts. (Daniel van Moll/NurPhoto/ Corbis via Getty Images)

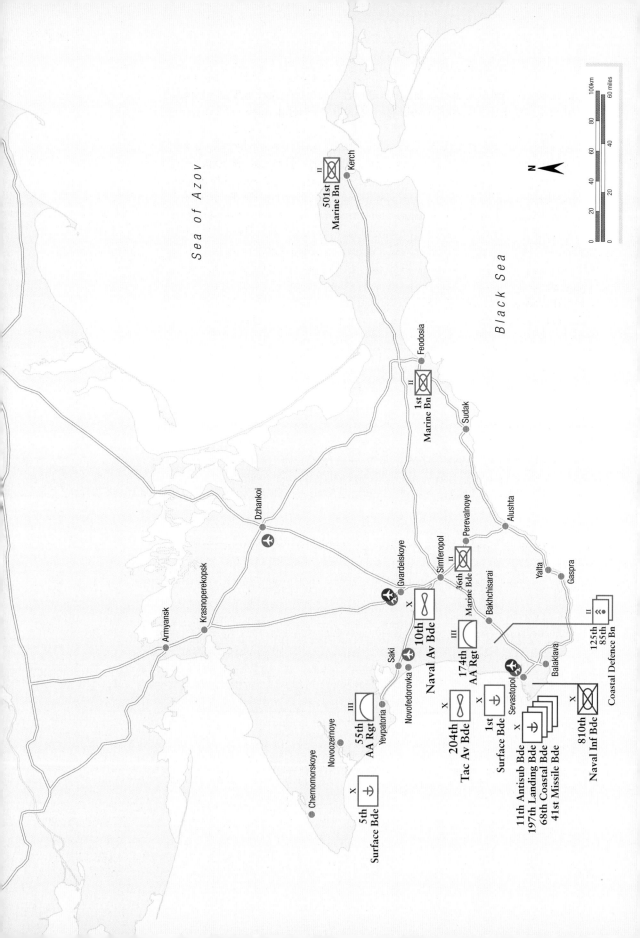

moved to a higher state of readiness, and forces began to be brought in, again under the pretext of regular force rotations – even though, had anyone been paying attention, they would have noted that while new troops were arriving, none seemed to be leaving.

Nonetheless, while the Russian forces on Crimea were relatively capable, they certainly did not have the kind of advantage that would guarantee a quick victory in a straight fight, especially as Ukraine could reinforce its garrison more easily by land than Russia by sea and air. In total, there were almost 20,000 Russian military personnel present, but the sizeable majority were sailors and technical and logistical personnel. The fighting force comprised a Naval Infantry brigade and some Naval *Spetsnaz* commandos from the BSF's special forces unit, the 431st Naval Reconnaissance Special Designation Point (431st OMRPSN), amounting to fewer than 2,500 actual combat troops.

Conversely, some 26,000 Ukrainian military and security personnel were based on Crimea, more than a tenth of the total Ukrainian Armed Forces (ZSU). The navy accounted for 19,000, the air force 3,000, the army and other arms 4,000. Admittedly, at least 15,000 were not front-line combatants, and none were kept at a particularly high readiness. All the same, there was a brigade and three battalions of marines, as well as three brigades (really at battalion strength) and two battalions of paramilitary Interior Troops of Crimean Territorial Command of the Ministry of Internal Affairs (MVS) and a Border Guard battalion. This added more than 2,500 paramilitaries to the Ukrainian strength, and while primarily security rather

UKRAINIAN ARMY ORDER OF BATTLE, FEBRUARY 2014

Kyiv and Northern Ukraine:
1st Indep Tank Bde (Honcharivske)
30th Indep Mech Bde (Novohrad-Volynskyi)
72nd Indep Mech Bde (Bila Tserkva)
95th Indep Airmobile Bde (Zhytomyr)
26th Indep Artillery Bde (Berdychiv)
27th Indep Rocket Artillery Rgt (Sumy)
54th Indep Recon Bn (Novohrad-Volynskyi)
Western Ukraine:
24th Indep Mech Bde (Yavoriv)
51st Indep Mech Bde (Volodymyr-Volynskyi)
80th Indep Airmobile Bde (Lviv, Chernivtsi)
128th Indep Mech Mountain Inf Bde (Mukachevo)
8th Indep Special Forces Rgt (Khmelnytskyi)
15th Indep Rocket Artillery Rgt (Drohobych)
39th Indep Air Defence Missile Rgt
   (Volodymyr-Volynskyi)
Central Ukraine:
17th Indep Tank Bde (Kryvyi Rih) (in the process of
   being disbanded)

28th Indep Mech Bde (Chornomorske)
3rd Indep Special Forces Rgt (Kirovohrad)
79th Indep Airmobile Bde (Mykolaiv)
107th Indep Rocket Artillery Rgt (Kremenchuk)
Eastern Ukraine:
25th Indep Airborne Bde (Dnipropetrovsk)
93rd Indep Mech Bde (Dnipropetrovsk)
92nd Indep Mech Bde (Kharkiv)
74th Indep Recon Bn (Dnipropetrovsk)
55th Indep Artillery Bde (Zaporizhia)
Crimea:
36th Indep Mech Coastal Defence Bde (Perevalnoye)
1st Indep Naval Inf Bn (Feodosia)
501st Indep Naval Inf Bn (Kerch)
These were largely paper units as of early 2014, and typically only one battalion per brigade was truly mobile and operational, although airborne, marine and special forces units were in a less threadbare state.

RUSSIAN ORDER OF BATTLE IN CRIMEA BEFORE THE INVASION

810th Indep Guards Order of Zhukov Naval Inf Bde
   (Simferopol)
880th Indep Naval Inf Bn
542nd Indep Naval Inf Air Assault Bn
557th Indep Naval Inf Bn
885th Indep Naval Inf Bn
888th Indep Naval Inf Recon Bn
113th Indep Naval Inf Tank Bn

1613th Indep SP Arty Bn
1616th Indep Rocket Arty Bn
547th Indep AA Bn
1622nd Indep AT Co
u/i Sniper Co
u/i detachment of the 431st Naval Reconnaissance
   Special Designation Point

The Black Sea Fleet was one of Russia's more combat-ready, in part due to its taking part in regular exercises such the *Kavkaz* (Caucasus) series. Here two Project 1171 (Tapir-class) landing ships (with the NATO reporting name 'Alligator') approach the Crimean coast, covered by Mi-8M (Mi-17) assault helicopters. (VASILY MAXIMOV/AFP via Getty Images)

than combat personnel, they were nonetheless armed with light personal and support weapons and some armoured vehicles.

While many of these elements – especially the Naval Infantry – were relatively well trained by the standards of the Ukrainian military, they were all subject to the disruption and demoralization caused by years of under-funding. The crucial issue, though, would be the lack of clear orders and, according to some, wilful confusion in the chain of command by officers hostile to the new regime, once the Russians made their move. Even so, from the first the Russian approach was to avoid direct confrontations, and instead to isolate, blockade and subvert these units, especially while they were so few in comparison with the Ukrainians.

THE OPERATION

As near as we can tell, the final 'go/no go' decision was made on 23 February, by Putin himself. *Vremya Cha* – zero hour – was set for 4am on 27 February. Meanwhile, the situation on the ground had become increasingly tense, something that would likely have happened even without Moscow's behind-the-scenes interference, but which the Russians certainly helped along. While Crimean Prime Minister Anatoly Mohyliov said that his government would accept the new government in Kyiv, thousands marched in the streets both against and in support of the Euromaidan. It did not help that the new government had decided to revoke the law that made Russian a second official language in regions such as Crimea. This was a political blunder, too easily characterized as proof that they were hostile to the Russian-speakers of south-eastern Ukraine and planned an enforced 'Ukrainianization'.

Crowds waving the Russian tricolour and the blue-and-yellow Ukrainian flag stand face to face in central Simferopol. The early demonstrations were peaceful, but this soon changed once tempers flared and Russian agents provocateurs had begun their work. (Sean Gallup/ Getty Images)

UKRAINIAN FORCES IN CRIMEA

Naval Infantry		Feodosia	47th Indep Interior Troops *Tyhr*	
Feodosia	1st Indep Naval Inf Bn		(Tiger) Rgt	
Kerch	501st Indep Naval Inf Bn	Gaspra	18th Indep Motorized Police Bn	
Perevalnoye	36th Indep Mech Coastal Defence Bde	Kerch	Co, Crimean Berkut Bde	
Sevastopol	56th Indep Guards Bn	Sevastopol	Co, Crimean Berkut Bde	
	25th Indep Coastal Defence Missile Bn		42nd Indep Interior Troops Rgt	
	85th Indep Coastal Defence Missile Bn	Simferopol	Co, Crimean Berkut Bde	
	801st Anti-Diversionary Detachment		9th Indep Interior Troops Bde	
Simferopol	406th Indep Arty Bde Group	*Lavanda* (Lavender) Special Operations Co		
Air and Air Defence		*Grifon* (Griffin) Special Judicial Police Bn		
Bakhchisarai	174th Air Defence Missile Rgt	*Sokol* (Falcon) Special Police Rapid Response Unit		
Belbek	204th Tactical Aviation Bde	Yalta	Co, Crimean Berkut Bde	
Derhachi	174th Air Defence Rgt	Yevpatoria	Co, Crimean Berkut Bde	
Feodosia	50th Air Defence Rgt		15th Indep Interior Troops Bn	
Yevpatoria	55th Air Defence Rgt	*Border Guards and Sea Guard*		
Navy		Balaklava	5th Sea Guard Squadron	
Donuzlav	5th Surface Ship Bde		Marine Security Squad	
	8th Indep Supply Ship Bn	Kerch	23rd Sea Guard Squadron	
Novofedorovka	10th Naval Aviation Bde	Yalta	Marine Security Squad	
Sevastopol	1st Surface Ship Bde	*Security Service of Ukraine*		
	18th Indep Supply Ship Bn	Sevastopol	Directorate A (Alpha) Regional	
	28th Indep Search & Rescue Bn		Directorate special operations team	
MVS Interior Troops		Simferopol	Directorate A (Alpha) Regional	
Balaklava	*Tin* (Shadow) Co, intelligence unit		Directorate special operations team	
	Kobra (Cobra) Bn			

At this stage, some officials in Crimea began to sound a note of alarm. Several naval commanders reported back to Kyiv that they had noted heightened levels of surveillance from what they presumed to be Russian intelligence officers and assets. In the SBU, there seems to have been a partial awareness of the extent to which Moscow was stirring up trouble and even bringing in weapons to arm its local allies. However, the head of the peninsula's SBU office, Pyotr Zima, appears to have watered these reports down before passing them to Kyiv. Given that he later defected to the Russians, it is an open question as to whether he had already been recruited by Moscow. In any case, the truth of the matter is that the new government in Kyiv was in such disarray at the time that even had the warnings been heeded, it is not certain much could have been done, especially as – on paper – Ukraine's forces in Crimea appeared quite formidable (*see* box).

On 23 February, perhaps 50,000 people rallied in Sevastopol under the banner of 'the People's Will against fascism in Ukraine'. It was noteworthy that in their number, especially providing security for ringleaders, were Cossacks and members of the Night Wolves motorcycle club. The protesters announced that they were setting up a rival local government and elected by acclamation Alexei Chaly as 'People's Mayor'. A local businessman and Russian citizen, Chaly began to form a new administration and also to set up a 'local self-defence militia'. Many of the local police, including the Crimean Berkut units (which had defied orders to disband) pledged their support for this rebel administration.

The formation of these 'people's squads' began right away, and more than 2,000 locals signed up there and then. Although in practice many of these volunteers were simply carried away with the enthusiasm of the moment, there was a core of perhaps 500 potential fighters, drawn disproportionately from the pro-Moscow Russian Unity party. More importantly, the presence of local militias provided a cover for Moscow to draft in a range of volunteers and deniable agents from outside Crimea, from Cossacks to veterans of the Soviet war in Afghanistan (*see* box) to thugs from the peninsula's underworld.

The contrast between the well-armed but also professional and disciplined 'polite people' of the Russian special forces, and their 'grey zone' allies, is evident in this photo of men outside Simferopol International Airport. The local allies, one wearing the orange-and-brown ribbon of St George that became considered a symbol of Russian military valour, were often of questionable military effectiveness, but helped confuse the nature of the operation. (Sean Gallup/ Getty Images)

A growing tension

This was a complex political environment, though. While ethnic Russians were marching to Moscow's tune, Crimean Tatars, including many whose families had been deported by Stalin and had only later returned to their homes, were rallying against any moves back to Russian control, and they represented around an eighth of the total population. They demonstrated their willingness to resist any drift towards Moscow. When protesters stormed the local mayor's office in Kerch, to the east of the peninsula, and tried to take down the national flag, Tatars joined the building's defenders, for example. So far, though, no weapons were in sight and the outcome was just a brawl, which ended with the blue-and-yellow Ukrainian flag still flying. If anything, the Tatars saw this moment of political chaos as an opportunity to push their own agenda. Their representative body, the Mejlis, gathered to oppose Chaly's shadow administration and demanded that all Crimea's monuments to Lenin, leader of the 1917 Bolshevik

AFGANTSY IN CRIMEA

The *afgantsy* – veterans of the ugly ten-year Soviet invasion of Afghanistan – played a significant role in Russia's domestic and foreign wars, from helping foil a hard-line coup in 1991 to supplying fighters in Ukraine's Donbas conflict. Often motivated by a muscular nationalism and sense of historic grievance, they proved a useful source of experienced and deniable fighters in Crimea. On 28 February, Frants Klintsevich, head of the Union of Veterans

of Afghanistan (and a long-time friend of Defence Minister Shoigu) flew to Crimea with 170 other *afgantsy* on board a military Il-76 transport aircraft. Many of them were former VDV paratroopers or *Spetsnaz*, and were issued weapons on their arrival. They would provide a reliable cadre within the local militias, not least there to keep some of their more unruly elements (such as gangsters) in line.

One of the most widely used APCs in the Russian take-over was the amphibious BTR-82 and, as here, the more modern BTR-82A. Widely issued to the Naval Infantry, the BTR-82A mounts a 30mm 2A42 autocannon. (ALEXEY DRUZHININ/AFP via Getty Images)

Revolution, be demolished within ten days. More than anything else, this was considered a symbolic act – a real break with the Soviet past – and a test of their strength.

One such statue was demolished by persons unknown that night, but the next day saw frantic conversations and negotiations between movers and shakers across the political spectrum, from Sergei Aksyonov, head of the Russian Unity party, to Oleg Tyagnibok, head of the Ukrainian nationalist Svoboda (Freedom) movement. Everyone agreed the situation was potentially explosive, but no one truly knew who would win if push came to shove. Vladimir Yatsuba, head of the Sevastopol city administration, stepped down, and half-hearted attempts by the SBU to arrest Chaly were foiled by a crowd of his supporters. Nonetheless, when acting Interior Minister Arsen Avakov returned to Kyiv after a brief fact-finding mission to Crimea, he airily claimed that the SBU and MVS had everything under control, and 'some negative movements by Russian troops in Sevastopol had been brought back to normal'.

In fact, Kyiv had lost control of the situation. Chaly's supporters forced Sevastopol council to make him chair of a new 'city coordination council' – even though no one really knew what this was – and in response, Ukrainian nationalists themselves began to mobilize on their own initiative. Igor Mosiychuk, a convicted terrorist who had since been amnestied, spoke on the behalf of the ultra-nationalist Right Sector movement when he went on television to warn that 'attempts to break the territorial integrity of Ukraine will be punished severely. If the authorities are not capable of this, then the Right Sector will... go to the Crimea.'

Police stand guard outside the Crimean regional parliament building. Most were locally recruited and either sympathized with the pro-Moscow forces or decided in any case to go with the flow and remain in Russian service after the annexation. (Sean Gallup/Getty Images)

After all, the new Ukrainian government was indeed in no shape to act. It only appointed a defence minister, Admiral Ihor Tenyukh, on 27 February, while the existing Chief of the General Staff, Admiral Yuri Ilyin, was already under suspicion, having been appointed by deposed President Yanukovych. In any case, he would be hospitalized by a heart attack that same day. The police in Crimea were in the main sympathetic to the pro-Moscow forces or else unwilling to take sides (most would later defect to the new government), and the military garrisons did not have one single loyal commander to coordinate their operations and, more to the point, no clear orders from up the chain of command. In such circumstances, even distributing live ammunition except under direct attack could conceivably have been considered mutiny.

The hidden hand

In the best of circumstances, this would have been a time of tense negotiations and fiery rhetoric. However, genuine rivalries and political opportunism were also being aggravated by Russian agents. Sometimes, this was quite overt. Late on 24 February, a group of Russian parliamentarians arrived in Simferopol. The delegation was headed by Leonid Slutsky, a leading light within the ultra-nationalist Liberal Democratic Party of Russia, and he immediately began meeting pro-Moscow politicians such as Aksyonov, promising them Moscow's support – using force if necessary – if they wanted to break with Kyiv.

Others were more covert. Russian Defence Minister Sergei Shoigu had sent Oleg Belaventsev to Crimea as his eyes, ears and, when necessary, strong right hand. A vice admiral in the Soviet navy who was later suspected of working for the KGB, Belaventsev had gone on to work closely under Shoigu first when he was Minister for Emergency Situations and then governor of the Moscow region. When Shoigu became Defence Minister, he made Belaventsev the general director of Slavyanka, a commercial company under the ministry's control. Belaventsev – who would later become the Presidential Representative to the Crimean Federal District – seems to have been there to coordinate between the Russian troops and their local auxiliaries, encouraging recruitment, paying

A Russian Mi-24 gunship flies over a landing ship moored in Sevastopol harbour. (VIKTOR DRACHEV/AFP via Getty Images)

IGOR 'STRELKOV' GIRKIN

While many of the influential figures within Russian nationalist circles confine themselves to espousing extreme positions in print or on TV and relying on other people to put themselves in harm's way, Igor Girkin – better known by his callsign 'Strelkov' or 'Strelok' – undoubtedly put ideas into action. After serving in the military, he volunteered to fight alongside Bosnian Serbs in the Yugoslav Civil War and pro-Moscow Russians in Moldova. Then, in 1996, he joined the FSB's own special forces. He served in both Chechen Wars, and was accused of involvement in war crimes, including the 'disappearance' of suspected militants. A keen military re-enactor, who favours playing the part of a tsarist officer, he left the FSB with the rank of colonel in 2013 and joined Konstantin Malofeyev's Marshall Capital Partners as a head of security. It is unclear whether he was still on Malofeyev's payroll when he led one of Crimea's 'self-defence' militias,

including handling some surrender negotiations with Ukrainian forces. After all, although he never made the claim himself, he was widely regarded within the militias as a direct representative of the FSB's. He would later take a small force into the Donbas and seize the city of Sloviansk, in his words 'pulling the trigger' of that conflict. He briefly became 'Defence Minister' of the rebellious Donetsk and Luhansk 'People's Republics', where he was implicated in other war crimes, before being dismissed at Moscow's demand when the Kremlin decided not to annex these regions after all. He since became an outspoken critic of Putin's, especially following the 2022 invasion, claiming that for all his posturing as a defender of Russian interests, he is too corrupt and incompetent to advance the nation's interests. Girkin is under sanctions throughout the West for the role he played in the Donbas conflict, and especially the shooting down of the airliner MH17.

out secret 'black budget' funds and overseeing the distribution of the weapons that they would shortly be toting openly on the streets.

Not to be outdone, the infamous Federal Security Service (FSB), which had long maintained connections with the Crimean underworld, began to broker deals with local gangsters. In part this was thanks to introductions made by Solntsevo, one of Russia's largest organized crime groupings, and one that had survived and prospered by knowing when to reach its own understandings with the authorities. The two main gangs on the peninsula, Salem and Baskaki, were persuaded to set aside their long-standing and often murderous differences. They would provide local intelligence and, more importantly, men on the ground, as provocateurs to stir up trouble and then play the part of pro-Moscow local militias.

More broadly, the FSB encouraged Russian nationalists to reach out and assist their allies on the peninsula. In particular, Russian millionaire Konstantin Malofeyev, well known for his strong nationalist and Orthodox religious beliefs, sent two of his own people to Crimea. One was Alexander Borodai, a PR consultant who began helping Aksyonov and his Russian Unity party in their political campaign. The other was a senior security officer from his Marshall Capital Partners company. This was Igor Girkin, who would later become better known by his callsign Strelkov ('Shooter'), a former colonel in the FSB, who began organizing volunteers to form armed squads for when it was time to strike, as well as quietly reaching out to police officers whom the FSB and its local allies had assessed as potential defectors (*see* box).[4]

---

4 Malofeyev, Borodai and Girkin are all under British, US and European Union sanctions for their role in the Ukrainian conflict, although Malofeyev has denied the charges made against him.

The Crimean operation came too soon to be coordinated through the high-tech new National Defence Management Centre (NTsUO) being built at that very time, but did contribute to the fine-tuning of the capabilities it would eventually give. Instead, everything from the military deployments to the deniable activities of Defence Ministry representatives such as Oleg Belaventsev was handled through the old Central Command Post of the General Staff, for which Crimea was the last hurrah. (MIKHAIL KLIMENTYEV/ SPUTNIK/AFP via Getty Images)

Preparations for conquest

Meanwhile, regular Russian forces were preparing, under the cover of large-scale exercises and 'snap inspections' across the Western and Central Military Districts, which were initiated on 26 February and meant to last for the next few days. It was announced that by 28 February, the Western Military District's 6th and 20th Armies, the Central Military District's 2nd Army, and the Airborne Troops would all be involved, for a total of some 150,000 soldiers. Meanwhile, the Black Sea Fleet would also be involved, to maximize the confusion and the scope to conceal the preparations for invasion. As early as the night of 22–23 February, the VDV's *Spetsnaz* force, the 45th Independent Regiment, was brought to full readiness under the cover of one of these 'snap inspections' and moved from its base at Kubinka, near Moscow. Most went to the Russian airbase of Anapa, just 30 miles from the eastern tip of the Crimean Peninsula. A few, along with elements from the 16th *Spetsnaz* Brigade, were covertly deployed directly into the naval

A key role in the operation was played by the new KSSO Special Operations Command. The KSSO operator is part of the contingent sealing the Ukrainian base at Perevalnoye in early March. He is in the latest *Ratnik* kit, and in what looks a little like overkill, is armed with an SVD Dragunov sniper rifle slung on his back and a VSS Vintorez suppressed sniper rifle on his front. (Sean Gallup/Getty Images)

base at Sevastopol under cover of routine troop rotation. Paratroopers from the 76th Pskov Airborne Assault Division arrived at Novorossiysk on the Black Sea coast, and some would soon also find themselves in Sevastopol.

The new Special Operations Forces Command (KSSO), which had only been established in 2011–13 as Russia's answer to the US 1st Special Forces Operational Detachment (more commonly known as Delta Force) and Britain's SAS, was also being prepared for action. The Crimean operation would prove crucial for them,

THE SPECIAL OPERATIONS FORCES COMMAND

While Russia's *Spetsnaz* 'special designation' or 'special purpose' troops are generally labelled as 'special forces', they are really better thought of as relatively elite reconnaissance and light infantry troops, certainly a cut above regular Russian motor-rifle units, but not comparable to 'Tier One' Western operators. It was precisely because they felt a need for such a capability that in 2011, a new Special Operations Forces Command (KSSO: *Komanda Sil Spetsialnovo Naznacheniya*) was established at a base at Senezh, north-west of Moscow. Formally announced in 2012, this was to be built on the basis of the 346th *Spetsnaz* Brigade, as a strategic-level asset, trained and structured for covert and high-risk operations both within and outside Russia's borders. Along with its operational command headquarters at Senezh (Unit 99450), It also acquired facilities for its three main battalion-strength forces (Units 01355, 43292, 92154) at Kubinka-2, west of Moscow, where the VDV's 45th *Spetsnaz* Brigade is also based. The goal was to have it fully operational before the start of 2014, so that it was available in case of terrorist attacks on the 2014 Winter Olympics in Sochi, but this fortuitously meant it was also ready for Crimea. It had its first proper deployment in the seizure of the peninsula, and went on to play a key role in operations in Syria and Ukraine.

both in demonstrating their capabilities but also in giving them something of a cult status in Russia – and one that would ensure they found themselves at the forefront of future operations, from Syria to the 2022 invasion of Ukraine.

With the local authorities increasingly under the control of pro-Moscow forces, matters began to come to a head. On 25 February, a rally outside the council offices in Simferopol denounced the 'Revolution of Dignity' as an illegitimate coup, and Vladimir Konstantinov, speaker of the Crimean parliament, warned that the self-proclaimed 'Armed Forces of the Autonomous Republic of Crimea' would resist any attempts by Kyiv to impose its authority on the peninsula.

Naval Infantry of the Black Sea Fleet had already taken up positions in Sevastopol and at Simferopol Airport, blandly asserting that they were only there to guard Russian facilities. Moscow was able to defend this by claiming that the situation on the ground was getting out of control. On cue, the next day, competing rallies by the Tatars and the 'Russian Community of Crimea' clashed in central Simferopol. More than 30 people were injured and two died, and when Tatars tried to storm the administrative offices, the police weighed in against them. The pro-Moscow 'people's squads' declared that they were ready to resist the attempt to 'export Kyiv's coup' to Crimea. However, it was noted that among the more violent and provocative of the pro-Moscow crowd were gangsters from Salem

Another hangover from the Soviet times was the reliance of both sides on the durable Il-76 heavy-lift aircraft. This is a Ukrainian Il-76 engaging in a prisoners-of-war swap with the separatist self-proclaimed Donbas republics at the Boryspil International Airport. (Maxym Marusenko/NurPhoto via Getty Images)

and Bashkaki, who had put their usual rivalries aside under their deal with the FSB.

The scene was set for intervention. On 26 February, ten Il-76 transport aircraft brought more paratroopers from the 76th Division to Simferopol, while Russian troops began snap inspections in the Western and Central Military Districts bordering Ukraine. The aim of this latter move was two-fold. In the short term, they provided a cover for troop movements into and near Crimea. Afterwards, the build-up of forces around eastern Ukraine would represent an implicit threat, a warning to Kyiv not to try to intervene in the peninsula.

Vremya Cha

At just after 0400 on 27 February, while Belaventsev was ringing round local 'people's squad' commanders to get their men on the streets, Russian troops began rolling from their bases in GAZ STS *Tigr* (Tiger) LMVs, trucks and APCs. They wore no insignia, their faces hidden under balaclavas. They refused to answer questions as to who they were, or simply described themselves as members of 'Crimea's armed self-defence forces'. Yet they were disciplined and professional, carried the latest Russian small arms and were equipped with the new *Ratnik* personal equipment suite (*see* box) that had only been issued in 2013. For all that, Moscow flatly denied any involvement. Indeed, even in March, when Putin was asked if they were Russian soldiers, he asserted – admittedly with a smirk – that they were local militias 'who may have acquired their Russian-looking uniforms from local military shops.' The author, who was in Moscow at the time, dutifully checked the local *voyentorg* military shops and second-hand army surplus suppliers – and found there was a distinct absence of *Ratnik* gear to be found, to no great surprise.

In hindsight, this all seems like a transparent and familiar ruse. However, such was the confusion at the time and the bland certitude of Russian government spokespeople that there was genuine uncertainty in both Kyiv and the West. Were these so-called 'little green men' (whom the Russians would come to call *vyezhliviye lyudi*, 'polite people', after their disciplined demeanour), not government forces but mercenaries? Could it be a maverick operation by the Black Sea Fleet command, without Moscow's sanction? This confusion was enough to give the Russians crucial hours, in some cases days, in which to establish commanding positions across the peninsula.

First of all, they joined up with various local militias and took the Supreme Council and Council of Ministers buildings in central

To have moved large amounts of heavy equipment to Crimea before the operation would have been an obvious warning, so the initial movements of Russian forces relied heavily on trucks, commandeered civilian vehicles and the GAZ-2330 *Tigr* (Tiger) LMV. The *Spetsnaz* especially appreciated its mobility and flexibility, as in the case of this team mounting an impromptu roadblock. (Bulent Doruk/Anadolu Agency/Getty Images)

THE *RATNIK* PERSONAL EQUIPMENT SUITE

In common with many Western armies, the Russians have been keen to acquire an integrated future infantry combat system including modern battle dress, body armour, communications and night vision systems, and survival gear. The result was *Ratnik* (Warrior), first introduced in 2013, although batch production only began in 2015. Including ten subsystems and 59 individual items, it represents a substantial step forward for Russian soldiers, even if distribution to non-elite forces has been slower than planned, and certain components such as a night-vision monocular ended up only issued to very few personnel. It includes 6B45 body armour, with *Granit* (Granite) rigid insert plates and a 6B47 composite helmet, and is meant to be integrated with the *Strelets* (Musketeer) voice and video communications system. Variants exist for specialist troops, with paratroopers receiving lighter 6B46 armoured vests, for example.

Simferopol. The handful of police on duty at that early hour either stood aside in the face of this overwhelming superiority in firepower or actively joined the 'people's squads'. The Russian forces, some 30 KSSO operators, soon supported by Naval Infantry and paratroopers of the 45th Regiment, secured the building, while the motley local auxiliaries began to set up barricades around the buildings and hoisted Russian flags.

The authorities were caught flat-footed. Crimean Prime Minister Anatoly Mogilev went on TV to try to reassure the population that everything was under control but that people ought to stay home while the situation was resolved. Meanwhile, the local MVS Interior Troops command went on alert, and more police were sent to cordon off the centre of Simferopol. In a few cases, there were clashes between the police and 'people's squads', with some of the latter breaking through to reinforce the defenders of the seized government buildings. However, the 'little green men' were both disinclined to pick a fight and too heavily armed for the police to be willing to tackle, so they maintained a careful neutrality.

Mogilev tried to open negotiations with them but was rebuffed. The Russians' real goal was to hold an extraordinary session of the legislature which would install a local government of their choice. While the KSSO operators held the chamber, local militiamen marshalled by Girkin were rounding up friendly or neutral parliamentarians, offering them safe passage to the chamber to vote the right way. Many were glad to oblige; others, faced by armed men who would not take no for an answer, swallowed their concerns. A vote was duly held by the 64 parliamentarians who had been assembled (out of the 75 total):

The motley nature of the 'people's squads' is evident in this picture of the cordon outside the Crimean parliament building. They are wearing everything from modern digital pattern battledress to Soviet-vintage 'amoeba' KLMK, with the orange-and-brown St George's ribbons one of the few standard features. By this time, though, they were all armed and some were wearing body armour, largely looted from military stocks. (Sean Gallup/Getty Images)

Russian Naval Infantry cover the area around the Crimean parliament building in Simferopol with their 7.62mm PKM machine guns. (Sean Gallup/Getty Images)

Mogilev was formally dismissed and replaced by Aksyonov. Crucially, the sitting deputies also agreed to hold a referendum on Crimea's future status. The outcome hardly seemed in doubt, as the legislature also asserted that the Euromaidan had been an 'unconstitutional seizure of power by radical nationalists with the support of armed gangs', such that it would henceforth 'take full responsibility for the fate of the Crimea'.

This represented the first stage of the political assimilation of Crimea into the Russian Federation, but pushing through a likely unconstitutional vote did not necessarily change the situation on the ground. There were, after all, still more than 25,000 Ukrainian soldiers and security officers on the peninsula. Neutralizing or co-opting them, and preventing Kyiv from being able to reinforce or replace them, was arguably even more important.

Bottling up the peninsula

At this early stage, the balance of power was overwhelmingly with Ukrainian government forces. The Russians had fewer than 3,000 deployable combat troops on the peninsula, and while most of them were relatively elite, they lacked much heavy equipment, even after the Ropucha-class large landing ship *Azov* had docked at Sevastopol on the afternoon of the 27th, with 300 soldiers from the 382nd Independent Naval Infantry Battalion, with their BTR-82A APCs. This was a BSF unit, but based in Temryuk, on the Taman Peninsula, in the neighbouring Krasnodar region.

As for the 'self-defence forces', most of them were more for show, good enough to man a barricade or intimidate civilians, but of little real value in proper fighting. There were some exceptions, though. The Berkut special police units were competent and disciplined. Girkin himself had raised a unit that he called '*Spetsnaz*', although their performance would belie this parallel with Russian special forces, especially as he initially had only 154 guns for the 200 or so men in his command. One noteworthy militia unit that did perform well, though, was Rubezh (Borderline), which exclusively recruited veterans from the Naval Infantry.

Masked Berkut riot police man a checkpoint on the Perekop Isthmus. The initial official pretence was that they were there to keep out Ukrainian nationalists from the Right Sector movement, and the sign on the barrier reads: 'Fascism Shall Not Pass!' (VIKTOR DRACHEV/ AFP via Getty Images)

A Russian soldier restrains a colleague who has just begun firing warning shots as Colonel Mamchur leads over 100 unarmed Ukrainian troops out of the Belbek airbase, in a bid to express a protest and open negotiations. Fortunately, the more jumpy or aggressive Russians were calmed down and a dialogue began. (Photo by Sean Gallup/Getty Images)

As mentioned above, on the morning of the 27th, Berkut forces had seized checkpoints on the roads leading into the peninsula as a precautionary measure, parking BTR-60PB APCs across the main highway and setting up machine guns and grenade launchers to cover the main access routes, ostensibly to prevent Right Sector militants from entering the peninsula. Once the pro-Russian forces had established their political control in Simferopol, though, the operation to establish physical control could begin in earnest. Even so, the intent at this stage was clearly to bottle up Ukrainian forces, not to engage in direct hostilities with them.

That evening, for example, more Russian troops accompanied by 'people's squads' seized Simferopol Airport and took up positions around Belbek Airport at Sevastopol, a Ukrainian military airbase housing two squadrons of MiG-29 fighters of the 204th Tactical Aviation Brigade. At first, the Russians contented themselves with controlling the access to and from the base, but on 3 March formally demanded the surrender of the base. The aforementioned commanding officer of the 204th Brigade, Colonel Yuly Mamchur, instead led his men out, unarmed and carrying their flag, towards the Russians and their allies. The Russians fired warning shots, but Mamchur continued towards them and formally rejected their demands. The Russians at this stage were under strict orders to avoid a violent confrontation, so he was allowed to lead his men back into the base. What followed was a genteel blockade for the next 20 days: unarmed Ukrainian troops in small numbers and out of uniform were allowed in and out of the base, but the Russians and the militias continued to maintain an outer perimeter. The hope appears

Colonel Yuly Mamchur, commander of the 204th Tactical Aviation Brigade, leads a column of his men out of Belbek airbase on 4 March. Mamchur became something of a national hero for his resistance to the Russians and capacity to hold his unit together. The blue cap bands denote air force troops, and the decision to bear forth the Soviet 'victory banner' as well as the Ukrainian flag was considered a powerful symbolic attempt to find some common ground with the invaders. (Sean Gallup/ Getty Images)

to have been that the government troops would eventually desert, defect or surrender, but while this did happen in some cases, Mamchur held the brigade together until the base was stormed on 22 March.

28 February

The next day, 28 February, saw the invasion begin in earnest. Up to 14 more Il-76 heavy-lifters delivered up to 1,500 more Russian troops to their Gvardeiskoye airfield near Simferopol. Eleven combat helicopters – three Mi-8 transports and eight of the latest Mi-35M gunship – landed at Kacha airbase, north of Sevastopol, which the Russians had been leasing. Meanwhile, more landing ships with not just troops but armour and artillery were setting out from Novorossiisk and also Anapa. The Ropucha-class large landing ships *Kaliningrad* and *Minsk* docked in Sevastopol late that day, carrying more troops, including men of the 10th *Spetsnaz* Brigade, while two more, *Georgy Pobedonosets* and the *Olenegorsky Gornyak*, set out late that evening and would arrive the next day bearing armoured vehicles, especially the increasingly ubiquitous *Tigr* LMVs.

Even the civilian Kerch ferry crossing became an informal invasion route, with trucks and minibuses bringing in dozens of armed volunteers, with no one daring to bar their way. They would then seize control of the Kerch border control point, disarming the existing customs officers and Border Guards.

Later, a tacit deal was struck: the customs officers would be left to their own devices, so long as they didn't actually try to do their jobs. By early March, the Russians were not making even a pretence of deniability and it seemed that every ferry was loaded with military vehicles (140 were counted entering Crimea illegally), but no attempt was made to stop them. As one of the customs officers later said, 'What the hell could we have done? There

THE COSSACKS

The Cossacks were originally semi-nomadic peoples living in the Dnieper, Don, Terek and Ural river basins in what is now Ukraine and southern Russia. Known for their independence of spirit, they were eventually incorporated into the Russian Empire and, for a while, the Polish–Lithuanian Commonwealth, by trading a degree of autonomy for military service. Known for their horsemanship, they were scouts, cavalry and, especially under late tsarism, enforcers of the will of the state, acquiring an unsavoury reputation for violent repressions. Their distinctive culture was virtually wiped out under Stalin, for all that there were still officially Cossack units and a rich theme of Cossack culture. In the 1980s, as the certitudes of Soviet ideology came into question, more and more people began rediscovering old traditions and identities, including that of the Cossacks.

In 1990s Russia, this became institutionalized, with special tax breaks for notionally Cossack businesses, Cossack private security firms, and attempts to create Cossack army units. A disproportionate number of the Russian citizens who call themselves Cossacks also espouse strong nationalist views. Many fought as volunteers in numerous regional conflicts alongside Russian troops or allies, including the Moldovan Civil War and the Chechen and Georgian Wars, and so it was hardly surprising that, with or without government encouragement, many would also head to Crimea. As it was, the Kremlin encouraged it, providing weapons, facilitating transport and offering Cossack security firms lucrative contracts in Crimea or elsewhere in Russia, if they were able to mobilize volunteers to go join the local 'self-defence forces'.

An unidentified Russian (whom some sources have suggested was an intelligence officer, although this is unconfirmed) watches as unarmed Ukrainians are marched past under guard. (Sean Gallup/Getty Images)

were four of us on duty with automatic pistols – were we going to hold up a tank?' Although for the sake of precision, most accounts spoke of the ferry just being used to bring in trucks, support vehicles and light armoured vehicles, along with four BM-21 Grad MLRS and six BTR APCs, probably BTR-80K command versions.

The disarray within the state apparatus also meant that others could even make their way across the land border into south-eastern Ukraine and from there to Crimea unhindered, as long as they were unarmed. Many members of the Kuban Cossack Army (*see* box) used this route and were welcomed across the Perekop Isthmus, with weapons waiting for them.

Controlling access to the peninsula was clearly a priority. 'Little green men' seized the offices of Krymaerorukh, the company that provided air traffic control services across Crimea's airspace. According to the SBU, the Russians were assisted by Simferopol Airport's deputy director, who gave them access to both the airport and Krymaerorukh. A former Ukrainian military officer, he was apparently recruited – likely by the GRU – as far back as 2011, and his case illustrates a recurring problem for Kyiv. Not only were the authorities dealing with a peninsula in which many of the locals were genuinely hostile to the central government and supportive of the idea of re-joining Russia, but this was also a theatre in which Moscow's intelligence agencies had been busy recruiting assets for years. As one SBU

Ukrainian marines in their base in Feodosia, while outside a Russian soldier looks on from the vantage point of his APC, parked right in front of the main gate. (Kyodo News Stills via Getty Images)

officer later ruefully put it: 'We were outgunned in the "shadow war" just as much as we were on the ground.'

Other soldiers took position around Saki airbase at Novofedorovka just north of Belbek, the only Ukrainian Naval Aviation facility in Crimea. As well as the now-redundant NITKA (*Nazyemny Ispitateiny Treynirovochny Kompleks Aviatsii*), the Soviets' only shore-based aircraft carrier flight training and test site, it was home to two squadrons of the 10th Saki Naval Aviation Brigade: one of ageing Be-12 'Mail' seaplanes (which could not actually land at sea, because the resin seals in their boat-like underbellies had decayed) and one of various rotor-wing craft, including Kamov Ka-29 assault ships and Ka-27 and Mi-14 anti-submarine helicopters. Again, though, the Russians appeared in no rush. On 3 March, four helicopters and three planes – all that were flightworthy – were able to escape from the airbase; no moves were made to shoot them down. Only two days later did Russian troops drive Kamaz trucks onto the base, parking them across its runway to prevent the remaining Be-12s from taking off.

Armed crewmen of the naval command ship *Slavutych* stand on guard even though, in the earlier stages of the operation, the Russians were largely happy to blockade the ports and wait for the Ukrainians to surrender. (Sean Gallup/Getty Images)

At the same time as Novofedorovka was being blockaded, four GAZ *Tigr* jeeps carrying a platoon from the Russian 810th Naval Infantry Brigade drove up to the main entrance to the Sea Guard – Ukrainian coast guard – base at Balaklava, south of Sevastopol. They did not try to force entry, but sealed the gate and posted snipers commanding the access points. Later that day, Captain First Rank Alexander Tolmachev, commander of the BSF's 41st Missile Boat Brigade, delivered a warning that by orders of a mythical 'Crimean Security Council', the Sea Guards should consider themselves confined to their base, allegedly to ensure that 'extremists' did not seize their weapons. To underline his point, one of his boats, the Tarantul III-class missile corvette *Ivanovets*, took up position at the mouth of Balaklava Bay, claiming that engine failure meant it could not be moved. Armed with four P-270 Moskit (Mosquito) anti-ship missiles, a 76mm AK-176M rapid-fire gun, two 30mm AK-630M gatling close-in weapons systems, and a Strela-3M SAM launcher, the *Ivanovets* packed a considerable punch in its 56-metre (184ft) hull, and was more than enough to close the bay to any unfriendly traffic. Nonetheless, the sailors of the 5th Sea Guard Brigade, who had been anticipating just such a development, opted to put to sea, headed for Odessa. The *Ivanovets*, faced with the choice of either opening fire or letting them go, opted for the latter. They posed no serious threat, after all, and the Russians were trying to avoid escalation.

The peninsula was also sealed up on the information front. 'Little green men' took over state TV and radio centres, the Yalta TV and radio station and the local GTRK Krym station in Simferopol. Others seized facilities of OJSC Ukrtelecom, the national telecommunications provider, as well as the Crimean Internet Exchange Point. Telephone and internet

This view of a Tarantul-III class corvette clearly shows the P-270 Moskit anti-ship missile launchers that made the *Ivanovets* such a potential threat to the light Ukrainian ships. (Andrey Rudakov/Bloomberg via Getty Images)

connections with the mainland were virtually blocked. Nor were outside politicians and would-be mediators welcome. On the evening of the 28th, Ukrainian parliamentarian and future president Petro Poroshenko arrived in Simferopol with the intention of trying to open dialogue with his Crimean counterparts, but he was driven out by a vociferous mob of pro-Russian activists, in whose number some of the usual suspects from the Salem and Baskaki gangs were noted.

1 March and the 'Crimean Spring'

Although reinforcements were arriving, so far the thinly stretched Russian forces were to a large extent relying on bluff and confusion. This was another virtue of the 'self-defence forces' – though most of them might have been of questionable real value in a fight, the reports of their movements and numbers helped obscure quite how few the Russians still were and quite what they were doing. Meanwhile, Kyiv was also in disarray, with little real idea of the situation on the ground, and no clear response.

Many officials, such as SBU director Valentyn Nalyvaichenko, had no doubts from the outset that this was a Russian operation. Media accounts likewise presented this in stark terms. TV correspondent Roman Bochkala, for example, encapsulated the public mood when he noted:

> Negotiations are underway in the military units of Crimea. The Russian military has turned up and is demanding that commanders submit to the Crimean government. And given who heads it, in practice that means Moscow. The goal is to remove the army from Kyiv's control. The good news is that if this happens, there will be no war. The bad news: Ukraine will have lost Crimea.

However, Ukrainian Defence Minister Ihor Tenyukh was keenly aware that his army was simply unprepared for any kind of full-scale war with Russia. On paper, the army had a total strength of 41,000, but it emerged that only 6,000 of them were actually combat-ready, and these tended to be more lightly armed special forces, marines and paratroopers. Most of the available tanks at Kyiv's disposal were ageing and unmodernized T-64s, which were considered under-gunned and under-armoured in comparison with the modern Russian forces arrayed across the border. The air force was in an even worst state, with only 10 per cent of personnel combat-ready and 15 per cent of fixed- and rotary-wing aircraft deemed airworthy. Of the navy's vessels, only four were combat-ready – three of which had been docked at Crimea and were now blockaded. This left only the Project 1135.1 Nerei-class (NATO: Krivak III) patrol frigate *Hetman Sahaidachny*. Flagship of the Ukrainian fleet, the *Hetman Sahaidachny* had fortuitously been taking part in the European Union's EUNAVFOR anti-piracy mission and was refuelling in Greece on the way back when Russia made its move. In any case, she was essentially a patrol ship, hardly able to go toe-to-toe with the BSF.

Furthermore, the new government's Western allies were also counselling caution (something about which many Ukrainian officials and soldiers would later complain). Unable to reach any consensus, its options severely limited, and unwilling to make threats on which it knew it could not follow through, Kyiv ended up just pledging to try to reach some diplomatic resolution and advising its own military and security personnel on the peninsula to 'avoid succumbing to provocations'. The government also began discussing possible political concessions to Crimea, such as greater autonomy, apparently not realizing or wanting to accept that by now it was Moscow that was calling the shots.

So there was no real response outside the peninsula. What units in mainland Ukraine that could be mobilized for national defence were readied. The 3rd and 8th Special Forces Regiments were shifted to the Kharkiv region and the border with the Crimean region. There are reports that, in March,

The Ukrainian flagship *Hetman Sahaidachny* might have also been captured by the Russians, had Ukraine not for years cultivated links with the West through joint deployments and military exercises, a trend that only deepened after the Crimean annexation. Here, a Ukrainian soldier on the left armed with an AKS-74U assault carbine and a British Light Dragoon work together during the RAPID TRIDENT multinational military exercises in 2014. (Sean Gallup/Getty Images)

Two Ukrainian Su-27 fighters were able for a while to deter Russian reinforcements by air, but ultimately it would have taken direct combat operations to make a substantial impact on the situation in Crimea, and Kyiv accepted this was simply not a viable option. (Mykhaylo Palinchak/SOPA Images/LightRocket via Getty Images)

Vladimir Putin, here speaking at a concert marking the anniversary of the annexation of Crimea in 2022, for years was able to enjoy the popularity boost resulting from it. (Photo by Getty Images)

platoon-sized teams from the 8th were briefly inserted into Perevalnoye base, but as it became clear that the likelihood was that the base would fall, they were soon exfiltrated to the mainland. These claims have, however, never been confirmed.

In any case, none of this would have any impact on events in Crimea. At one point on the 28th, it had looked as if some of the handful of flightworthy Su-27 fighters in the 831st Tactical Aviation Brigade at Myrhorod airbase on the mainland were going to be scrambled in a bid to intercept incoming troop transports, something that would have triggered an uneven air war. Two were actually put in the air. For a while, this seems to have deterred the Russians from reinforcing Crimea by air. However, when no direct orders were forthcoming from the Air Force Command in Vinnytsia, the brigade was stood down. Even as late as 13 March, Colonel Yuly Mamchur, the commander of the 204th Tactical Aviation Brigade, whose base at Belbek airfield had been under siege for a fortnight, was demanding that Kyiv provide clear orders to its troops stranded across Crimea. Above all, he wanted the leadership to authorize the troops to use lethal force, if needed, in their defence. It would take five more days – and the death of a Ukrainian soldier – for this order to come, by which time it was too late.

In the first days of the operation, though, the Russians knew better than to force the issue. As a veteran paratrooper who had been in Simferopol later recalled, 'We knew that if we came in, guns blazing, then the Ukrainians would instinctively fire back. So we kept our distance, stopped them from deploying, and waited for backup.' By 1 March, that backup was arriving, and symbolically, Aksyonov issued a formal – if some would say, rather belated – appeal to Russia for protection: 'Recognizing my responsibility for the lives and security of the people, I request that Russia's President Vladimir Putin offer assistance in providing peace and order in the territory of the Autonomous Republic of Crimea.' He also ordered that all Ukrainian forces on the peninsula place themselves under his command.

In another piece of theatre, Putin formally petitioned the Federation Council, the upper chamber of the Russian legislature, for permission to deploy forces onto Ukrainian territory 'until the normalization of the socio-political situation in that country.' This was promptly and duly given by what is, after all, a body packed with government yes-men and proxies. Even before that rubber-stamp approval, Putin certainly had more of the forces on the ground he needed by then. There were *Spetsnaz* from the 10th Brigade and 25th Independent Regiment, more Naval Infantry, and also more volunteers: Cossacks, nationalists, additional Night Wolves and even their president, Alexander Zaldostanov (who had acquired his menacing nickname of 'the Surgeon' for the less than macho reason that he was once a cosmetic surgeon's assistant). Indeed, the growing logistical demands of this expanding force meant that the decommissioned Lazarevsky Barracks in Sevastopol, which had actually become a tourist attraction, was pressed back into service for this purpose.

By 1 March, the centres of the main cities, including Simferopol and Sevastopol, were wholly under the control of the Russians, the 'people's squads', or police who had accepted the appointment of Igor Avrutsky, formerly head of the Crimean police's organized crime department and acting Mayor of Feodosia, as the peninsula's chief of police.

Late on the evening of 2 March, a formal ceremony was held at the Crimean Council of Ministers building with the intention of establishing the fiction of an independent Crimean state security apparatus. Pyotr Zima, the head of the Crimean section of the SBU, was made head of the Crimean Security Service, while the heads of the existing police and border service, Sergei Abisov and Viktor Melnichenko, swore their allegiance 'to the people of Crimea'. Aksyonov claimed that the day marked Crimea's true autonomy, but in practice this represented Moscow's effective take-over of the peninsula's internal security forces.

Taking the navy

Another figure at that ceremony was Rear Admiral Denis Berezovsky, at the time acting head of the Ukrainian Navy, who was himself defecting and being made commander of a mythical 'Crimean Navy'. After all, the Russians now felt confident enough to begin to close their grip on the remaining Ukrainian military forces on the peninsula, and they would start by focusing on the navy. Many Ukrainians simply deserted or defected to the Russian side, which promised that they would keep their ranks and receive bonus payments. These included not one, but two acting commanders of the Ukrainian Navy. Vice Admiral Sergei Yeliseyev had been promoted to the position on 19 February, even though he had been born in the Moscow region, but when he sided with the Russians, he was dismissed, and on 1 May he was replaced by Rear Admiral Berezovsky. The next day, Berezovsky himself duly defected and began trying to encourage naval vessels to defect with him.

While there were at first no takers, Berezovsky, accompanied by a bodyguard of Russian Cossacks (some of whom were later alleged to be KSSO operators or other special forces, under cover), visited several naval

Russian warships stand at the entrance to the main harbour in Sevastopol, blocking the command ship *Slavutych* and the anti-submarine *Ternopil*. The large ship in the centre is the Russian Project 323V Lama-class seagoing armament transport *General Ryabikov*. (Sean Gallup/ Getty Images)

Newly appointed Ukrainian naval commander Serhiy Hayduk speaks in his blockaded headquarters on 3 March. (VIKTOR DRACHEV/AFP via Getty Images)

facilities and ships under anchor in an effort to sway them. His efforts may have been unsuccessful, but they were rewarded: like Yeliseyev, he would later be made a deputy commander of the Russian Black Sea Fleet.

Kyiv appointed Rear Admiral Serhiy Hayduk as acting commander of the Ukrainian Navy, and – third time lucky – he proved loyal. Hayduk was able to rally his subordinates against the immediate temptations of defection. Indeed, reportedly, after he spoke to an assembly of officers, they spontaneously began singing the national anthem. Nonetheless, that was about all he could do, effectively being confined to his offices in the naval headquarters in Sevastopol. On 3 March, Cossacks supported by some Naval Infantry had made a half-hearted effort to seize the building, but had been driven off by marine guards. Later, the electricity to the building was cut off, but only on 19 March did the Russians finally make a serious move to take the building. Hayduk was held by the self-appointed local security forces before being released by Moscow the next day and handed over to the Ukrainian government.

Some of the smaller ships belonging to the State Border Service's Sea Guard had been able to escape before Moscow closed its fist. As mentioned above, the 5th Sea Guard Brigade took their chances and fled their base at Balaklava and set for Odessa, despite the presence of a Russian missile boat. Later, 11 ships from the Kerch Sea Guard detachment sailed to Mariupol. In all, 23 Sea Guard patrol boats and cutters were able to make it to government-held ports without being intercepted, leaving only five in the hands of the Russians.

Moscow was willing to let the lightly armed Sea Guard boats go, but had no intention of being so lax with the larger ships of the Ukrainian Navy. Just after Berezovsky's defection, armed militiamen tried to seize the

The presence of Mil Mi-35M gunships gave the Russians a distinct tactical advantage, both on land and at sea. (VITALIY TIMKIV/AFP via Getty Images)

Slavutych, formerly the Gofri-class Soviet intelligence and auxiliary ship *Pridneprovie*, based on a fishing trawler hull. Launched in 1990, it had then been absorbed into the Ukrainian Navy as a command ship. This seems likely to have been a poorly-thought-through local initiative, and the attackers were easily repelled in what was more of a show of force and limited brawl.

The Russians seemed willing to give Berezovsky a little time, but when it became clear that his

An understandably dejected Ukrainian Navy officer is escorted from their headquarters after it was taken by 'little green men.' (Oleg Klimov/Epsilon/Getty Images)

efforts were fruitless, the BSF decided to take matters into their own hands. The key Ukrainian naval force was the 12-strong 5th Surface Ships Brigade at the Southern Naval Base in Novoözernye on Donuzlav Bay. They had remained at dock both because of a lack of orders from Kyiv and also the nearby presence of the Atlant-class cruiser *Moskva*, whose 16 P-1000 *Vulkan* supersonic anti-shipping missiles made it a formidable threat. However, the Kremlin was still eager to avoid a direct confrontation if possible, and on the night of 5 March, a five-ship task force led by the *Moskva* sank the decommissioned Kara-class cruiser *Ochakov* and the tugboat *Shakhtyor* at the mouth of the bay.

This effectively blockaded the Ukrainians, and eventually they would surrender, ship by ship. On 21 March, the Polnochny-C-class medium landing ship *Kirovohrad* and Natya-class minesweeper *Chernihiv* handed themselves over to the Russians. Emboldened, they took the initiative and the next day sent in a mixed force of BSF naval officers and marines and Crimean militia, peacefully seizing the Albatros-class (Grisha II in NATO designation) anti-submarine corvette *Vinnytsia*. Bit by bit, the Russians became more confident, and as a final act, on the evening of 25 March, they took the last remaining combat vessel, the minesweeper *Cherkassy*. Captain 3rd Rank Yuri Fedash had for the past three days been sailing around Donuzlav Bay precisely to avoid being an easy target and made two attempts to break out into the open sea, the second time almost being beached by a Russian warship. Speedboats had tried to get alongside and been driven off by smoke grenades and improvised explosive charges thrown from the *Cherkassy*'s deck, but ultimately for all the courage and ingenuity of its crew, the ship was doomed. Eventually, she was boarded by heavily armed Naval *Spetsnaz* in two Mi-35 gunships who rounded the crew up at gunpoint. All told, this meant the Russians had been able to capture all of the 5th Surface Ship Brigade vessels, also including the *Cherkassy*'s sister ships *Chernigov*, *Cherkasy* and *Genichesk*. Many would later be returned to Ukraine.

Meanwhile, the other Ukrainian Navy ships that had been blockaded were forced to surrender or were seized. The *Slavutych* was taken in a two-hour tussle in which Crimean militia backed by Russian Naval Infantry finally overpowered its crew. Two more Albatros-class corvettes, the *Lutsk* and the *Ternopil*, had been trapped in Streletska Bay by Sevastopol and Donuzlav, respectively. On 20 March, the *Lutsk* surrendered and the *Ternopil* was stormed by Rubezh, the Crimean militia unit recruited exclusively from former Naval Infantry. They used stun grenades and fired some warning shots, but no casualties were suffered on either side. The command ship *Donbas*, a converted Soviet Project 304 repair ship, surrendered on the 20th. On 22 March, it was the turn of Ukraine's only submarine, the ageing Project 641 (NATO designation Foxtrot) diesel-electric patrol boat *Zaporizhia*, although half its crew had already abandoned it. The *Zaporizhia* was in such poor shape that the BSF refused to incorporate it, and eventually offered either to return it to Ukraine or break it down for scrap.

By 26 March, all Ukrainian ships anchored off Crimea had been seized or surrendered. While Berezovsky had not managed to convince any crews to defect en masse beforehand, in many cases up to a half of the crews of these ships opted to join the BSF, and Rear Admiral Dmitry Shakuro, naval chief of staff, also took Moscow's shilling. The Ukrainian Navy, to most intents and purposes, was neutralized and Crimea's waters were Russian.

Phoney war and real deaths

On the morning of 2 March, the deputy commander of Russia's Southern Military District, accompanied by the deputy commander of the 810th Naval Infantry Brigade, had arrived at the barracks of the Ukrainian 1st Marine Battalion in Feodosia and ordered them to surrender within an hour. Their demand was rejected, but Kyiv's concern that its soldiers would start to hand over their weapons or even switch sides was obvious. That same day, the General Prosecutor's Office released a statement warning that 'Servicemen of the Armed Forces of Ukraine must remember that they swore allegiance to the Ukrainian people! Thus, if they submit to demands for the surrender of their weapons, military equipment or their places of deployment, this will be considered to be high treason with the corresponding legal consequences.'

Ukrainian marines, backed by a BMP-2 IFV, guard the main gate of their base at Perevalnoye on 2 March, after it had been surrounded by Russian troops. At this stage, the Russians were treating the blockade lightly, not interrupting supplies of power, food and water and allowing locals still to interact with them. (Sean Gallup/Getty Images)

As it was, in those early days, the Russians and their Crimean proxies had only limited success with the military. Although most police either actively switched sides or simply went with the flow, the majority of the Border Troops and Interior Troops refused to follow their commanders in defecting to the self-proclaimed Crimean government. However, the Russians were more concerned about the regular soldiers, and were willing to play a longer game. As one Ukrainian defence official later acknowledged, 'The [Russians] knew better than to force the issue – they wanted time, first to strengthen their military deployments but also to apply psychological pressure.'

What followed was therefore a period of blockade and negotiation. The Russians went out of their way to project confidence, sometimes replacing their forces around some bases with local militia and allowing soldiers to come and go, as long as they were unarmed and out of uniform. Russian and Ukrainian marines even played football in Kerch. After all, the Russians knew that the balance of power on the peninsula was shifting in their favour. Besides, while at the outset most soldiers were loyal to Kyiv and had no idea of deserting or defecting, over time, the isolation, frustration with the government and blandishments of the Russian negotiators were slowly bearing fruit.

The Russians were especially successful at winning over some units, like the 501st Independent Battalion at Kerch. Here a marine (evident from his black beret and striped black and white vest) engages in discussion with a local. (GENYA SAVILOV/AFP via Getty Images)

These were largely military and GRU officers. While they did not generally lead to any units surrendering en masse, their work did mean that when the Russians eventually did force the issue, many Ukrainian soldiers were willing to join and the rest had largely been convinced that resistance was futile. For example, when the 501st Independent Battalion at Kerch that had played football with the Russians capitulated on 20 March – a three-quarters' strength battalion surrendering to just 20 soldiers – fully two-thirds of its soldiers took this deal.

The strategy of tension had its risks, though. On 18 March, two Russian military vehicles carrying a platoon of Crimean militia with rifles and shotguns, reportedly commanded by Strelkov/Girkin, and accompanied by a masked team of Russian *Spetsnaz*, drove up to the gates of the 13th Photogrammetric Centre of the Central Military-Topographic and Navigation Administration on Kubanskaya Street in Simferopol. When the naval guards refused them entry, an altercation began, but one of the militiamen began trying to scale the wall into the base compound. He was spotted by Ensign Serhiy Kokurin, who was manning the facility's watchtower, who ordered him to desist. One way or the other, the argument escalated into a firefight.

Kokurin was fatally injured in the exchange, and Ukrainian Captain Valentin Fedun was wounded in the neck and arm. One Crimean militiaman, Ruslan Kazakov, was also killed, and another, Alexander Yukalo, was wounded. Kazakov, a decorated veteran of both the First and Second Chechen Wars, was a member of the Volgograd Cossacks, who had gone to Crimea as a volunteer in February. The centre's commander, Colonel Andriy Andryushyn, was captured and persuaded the last defenders, who had barricaded themselves on the first floor of the building, to give themselves up. In total, 18 Ukrainians were disarmed and detained.

Fedun and Yukalo were taken to hospital, and if anything the Russians seemed unhappy with how events had spiralled out of control. The Crimean Interior Ministry put out a story that the confrontation was sparked by some unknown third party, a sniper who had fired on both sides precisely as a provocation. This was an implausible tale but demonstrated how the Russians were keen to find an excuse to de-escalate. Symbolically, both Kokurin and Kazakov were given a formal funeral send-off together at the Simferopol House of Officers, attended by Aksyonov, and Girkin's militia unit was disbanded.

Nonetheless, this finally spurred the Ukrainian Defence Ministry formally to authorize its troops to use lethal force in their defence. It was too little, too late, though. Thereafter, the Russians seem to have been even more careful to avoid such confrontations – and made less use of the undisciplined militias – even though there would be two more casualties. As for Colonel Andryushyn, he ended up being another defector to the Russian side.

Those final casualties would come the next month. On 22 March, troops from, appropriately enough, the 10th *Spetsnaz* Brigade took the 10th Naval Aviation Brigade's Novofedorovka airbase. There was no real resistance at the time, and the Ukrainian soldiers and their families were sent to dormitories in Novofedorovka while they awaited being sent back to the mainland. On 6 April, a dispute broke out between some Ukrainian sailors and Russian *Spetsnaz*. Matters escalated to the point where Sergeant Yevgeny Zaitsev shot Major Stanislav Karachevsky of the Ukrainian Navy twice at point-blank range with his AK-74 rifle. Major Karachevsky died immediately, and Zaitsev was arrested and later sentenced to two years in prison by a military court.

Taking the bases

In any case, March saw Moscow closing its fist on the peninsula by picking off the remaining Ukrainian bases one by one. On 1 March, Russian troops in *Tigr* LMVs accompanied by a force of Cossacks in trucks drove onto the single runway of the Kirovskoye airfield in eastern Crimea, which was guarded by a company of Ukrainian marines from the 501st Independent Naval Infantry Battalion, with six BTR-80 APCs. The Cossacks took the lead, explaining that they were concerned that the base could be used by Kyiv to land troops and, as one of their spokesmen later put it, 'asked very nicely if they could secure it'. The marines

The BTR-80 is amphibious and versatile, but still a relatively thin-skinned APC and thus vulnerable to modern RPGs. (ATTILA KISBENEDEK/AFP via Getty Images)

surrendered, although they were probably swayed less by the Cossacks' manners as the presence of the masked Russian troops, who by this point were pointedly deploying RPG-28 *Klyukva* (Cranberry) AT launchers. Their 125mm tandem shaped-charge warheads, designed to burn through a metre of tank armour, would have made quick work of the BTR-80s' 10mm-thick hulls.

Day by day, facility by facility, the Russians moved in. On 2 March, the headquarters of the Crimean division of the Border Guards in Simferopol was taken. Then an air defence station on Cape Fiorent, near Sevastopol, as the Russians focused on the south-west of the Crimea. Then they moved to the rest of the peninsula. On 9 March, it was the 10th Naval Aviation Brigade base at Saki, outside Novofedorovka, although not before it had managed to move some of its aircraft to the mainland. The next day, it was the turn of the 222nd Automotive Battalion in Bakhchisarai and a battery of the 25th Independent Coastal Defence Missile Battalion in Chernomorsky. The anti-terrorist commandos of the MVS's 47th Tyhr (Tiger) Special Purpose Regiment – really little more than a company in strength – had been blockaded in their base in the village of Krasnokamenka outside Feodosia since the beginning of the month, with little food and no electricity. Lacking much in the way of heavy equipment beyond some aged RPG-7 AT rocket launchers and some equally antiquated BRDM-2 scout cars, when a company of Russian troops turned up, they quickly surrendered. Several, indeed, joined the occupiers, still angry at the loss of two of their number to unknown snipers' bullets while serving in Kyiv during the 'Revolution of Dignity'.

The psychological pressure of lengthy blockades, as well as the sense of isolation and a lack of clear orders from Kyiv, left many Ukrainian troops ultimately unwilling to fight against what soon seemed overwhelming odds. (Spencer Platt/Getty Images)

Most of these were relatively small facilities, and often essentially technical ones, like the radar station on Mount Ai-Petri (blockaded on 12 March, taken on the 15th) or the 55th AA Regiment in Yevpatoria (seized by *Spetsnaz* on 1 March). Their personnel were, after all, not trained, equipped or mentally prepared to resist what by then were overwhelming odds, given that the Russians could focus their efforts on the targets of the day. Besides, the messages they were getting from both Kyiv and Rear Admiral Hayduk did not encourage resistance. On 16 March, for example – just three days before he was captured and on a day when, by contrast, Ukrainian Prime Minister Arseny Yatsenyuk was warning 'all the instigators of separatism and division' that 'the ground under your feet will burn' – Hayduk was almost pleading with the Crimean authorities:

> I ask you to take all measures to cool down the 'hotheads,' so as to prevent a new round of confrontation… This is a time for reconciliation, for the work of politicians

and diplomats... I am sure: Ukrainian and Russian soldiers should not shoot at each other... I believe in the wisdom, prudence and endurance of the people of Crimea and Sevastopol.

This may have been diplomatic, but it was not exactly inspiring. One Ukrainian marine (who did not change sides) from the 1st Battalion later recalled the outrage with which he and his squad-mates greeted Hayduk's statement, saying that 'we were living with Moskali [a derogatory term for Russians, derived from Muscovite] outside our walls and windows, never knowing when they would next try and take us, and here was an admiral, calling for reconciliation when we wanted reinforcements!'

Nonetheless, often the process was, if anything, quite amicable, especially as the Russians were able to contrast themselves with local 'hotheads' in Hayduk's words to appear to be the Ukrainians' defenders, not their jailers. On 2 March, for example, Russian troops took up positions outside the 501st Naval Infantry Battalion's base in Kerch. Although a crowd of Crimean Tatars gathered, claiming to be willing to act as 'human shields', the Russian and Ukrainian marine commanders quickly reached an agreement whereby the Ukrainians would hold the base but the Russians would maintain a perimeter, without disrupting inward supplies of food or outward visits by soldiers into town. Indeed, as a symbol of this accord, the Ukrainian flag was lowered from the main gate, even though they did park BTR-70 APCs just inside the perimeter as a security measure. By the time the Russians had taken over the base on 20 March, at least a third of the battalion had already defected.

It was typically a combination of genuine disaffection on the part of some soldiers – even those not willing to defect felt that they had been abandoned by Kyiv – and also the psychological pressure of being isolated and blockaded for days. The result was that many facilities, especially those manned by non-combat personnel, typically surrendered at the first pressure. In the words of one Russian soldier:

[T]hey were not cowards, but nor were they suicidal. We'd roll up and look menacing, with assault rifles and RPGs, and that would give them the excuse to give up. We didn't look down on them, or treat them badly if they surrendered right away. The whole idea was that by the time we turned up, they were already ready, subconsciously ready, for us.

Not all the objectives would be so easily taken, though. The Russians believed that the most serious potential challenge would come from the elite 1st Independent Naval Infantry Battalion in Feodosia. Perhaps the most dangerous element of the 36th Independent Coastal Defence Brigade, headquartered in Perevalnoye, this unit was one of the few that was at anywhere near establishment strength, with some 1,800 marines, including some of the most experienced in Ukrainian service. Even so, in practice only a single battalion-strength group was truly combat-ready, and many of its 41 T-62BV tanks were out of service.

It had been blockaded by *Spetsnaz* since 2 March, but although up to half had either deserted or, in the main, defected to the Russians, a determined rump under Lieutenant Colonel Dmitry Delyatitsky remained. The decision was made to use a show of force. On 21 March, KSSO operators landed in their parade ground from Mi-8M helicopters, with two Mi-35s providing air cover. They proceeded to use GM-94 pump-action grenade launchers to fire stun and smoke grenades through the barracks windows. When some marines made to close with them, the operators

A Ukrainian soldier marine inside the blockaded Perevalnoye base. (Sean Gallup/Getty Images)

fired warning shots into the air, while two BTR-82As crashed through the compound gates and more troops joined the fray, accompanied by up to 80 militia. The Russians and Ukrainians alike were eager to avoid recourse to their firearms: the former wanted to avoid pushing remaining hold-outs into armed resistance; the latter knew that they could not prevail in a firefight. The result was a rolling and epic series of brawls that lasted a couple of hours, as the Russians worked their way through the barracks. Eventually, the base was taken, with no more than a lot of bruises and some broken bones on both sides. Lieutenant Colonel Delyatitsky himself, who had been at the forefront of the melee, suffered three broken ribs, but became something of a legend among Ukrainian and Russian soldiers alike.

Heartened by their success in Feodosia, the Russians turned to the other remaining tough nut: the 204th Tactical Aviation Brigade in Belbek. The next day, Russian Naval Infantry supported by six BTR-82As smashed their way into their compound through a concrete perimeter wall and forced them to surrender at gunpoint. The redoubtable Colonel Mamchur was taken prisoner, although he would soon be released with five other senior Ukrainian officers who refused to turn their coats, including Major General Igor Voronchenko, deputy commander of the Ukrainian Navy (who held an army rank as he was a marine officer – he would in 2016 be made vice admiral when he became overall navy commander).

KSSO TAKE ON THE 1ST BATTALION

When the KSSO were sent in to storm the barracks of the 1st Independent Naval Infantry Battalion in Feodosia on 21 March, they were under orders to avoid fatalities if at all possible and so hoped shock and surprise would be their best weapons. Here, operators are disembarking from a Mi-8M hovering low over the parade ground between barracks blocks, while one of their number is already preparing to fire stun or tear gas grenades into the buildings from his GM-94 grenade launcher. An officer, meanwhile, is making the first calls for surrender through a loudhailer. One of the two Mi-35 gunships assigned to provide top cover is making a deliberately low pass over the barracks, to add to the confusion. The operators are wearing full *Ratnik* kit, but most are not armed with their usual AK-74M rifles but Taran PR-T rubber truncheons, in anticipation of the desire to clear any die-hards from the barracks without, if possible, the use of lethal force. A second Mi-8M is waiting to deliver another squad of *Spetsnaz*, while reinforcements are even at this moment smashing their way in through the perimeter wall.

On 22 March, Russian special forces finally stormed Belbek airbase. Note the Vant-VM ballistic shield. (Photo by Oleg Klimov/Epsilon/Getty Images)

Digging in

The main route into Crimea from the mainland, the Perekop Isthmus, became the site of a face-off between Ukrainian troops and Border Guards, and the Russians. At first, the Berkut volunteers had controlled access, but in early March, fearing a possible Ukrainian incursion, Russian regulars established a reinforced checkpoint at the so-called Turkish Rampart, closer to the border with the Kherson region. This was expanded until it housed two platoons of troops, one mounted in APCs and the other in *Tigr* LMVs. In due course, this was handed over to the FSB Border Troops, but for months it represented the closest Russian military position to the Ukrainian lines. In mid-March, a battery of 2A65 Msta-B towed 152mm howitzers and another of BM-27 Uragan MLRSs were dug in to cover the isthmus.

The irony was that the Ukrainians were just as concerned about a Russian incursion. The State Border Service established three checkpoints along the border on the isthmus, in the villages of Chaplynka, Salkovo and Kalanchak, supported by mobile army and Interior Troop patrols. On 2 March, the 1st Battalion of the 79th Independent Airmobile Brigade was brought to combat readiness, as it was the only element of the brigade apart from its reconnaissance company that was fully manned by volunteers. It was deployed near Chaplynka in the Kherson region, close to the border with Crimea. There was a thought that it could move into Crimea to secure the north of the peninsula. However, when Major Dmytro Marchenko led a reconnaissance mission in a civilian vehicle, heading to Armyansk, he quickly saw that the road was being controlled by Berkut special police, so the plan was quickly abandoned. Eventually, once the conflict in the Donbas ignited, it was rotated eastwards, along with the elite 95th Independent Airmobile Brigade, which was also briefly sent to Kherson to resist a feared Russian advance.

On 11 March, the Ukrainian government decided to institute a partial mobilization, as well as to use the MVS Interior Troops as the basis for a new National Guard, as a parallel militarized force. However, it would take time for reservists and new recruits to be combat-ready, especially as the mobilization of the former was badly organized. In any case, precisely to deter any Ukrainian counter-offensive, the Russians also stepped up aggressive troop movements under the cover of exercises on Ukraine's eastern and north-eastern borders, involving some 10,000 soldiers. This was successful in getting Kyiv to divert some of the forces it could otherwise have sent south to shore up its eastern defences.

The only other direct connection between Crimea and the mainland is the Arabat Arrow, a long, narrow sandy spit of land 112km (70 miles)

Once the Russians began to receive substantial amounts of artillery and heavy armour, like this tank shown outside Simferopol, then any serious prospect of a Ukrainian counter-attack disappeared. Their key advantage would precisely have been if they had been able to mobilize and act when the invaders were both relatively few in number and lightly armed. (DMITRY SEREBRYAKOV/AFP via Getty Images)

long, and 8km (5 miles) at its widest, separating the Syash lagoons from the Azov Sea. Technically, only the southern half was considered Crimean with the northern half being part of the Kherson region. First, on 8 March, the Crimean militia set up a checkpoint in Solyane, the only settlement in the southern half of the spit, and later the Russians pushed their positions northwards. By the end of the year, though, they would have withdrawn to the former border between Crimea and Kherson.

Any prospect of a Ukrainian counter-strike was quickly dispelled when the 727th Independent Naval Infantry Battalion and the army's 18th Independent Motor Rifle Brigade, both with their full complements of artillery and armour, were brought in by sea from Kerch, with the latter quickly moving to secure the Perekop Isthmus. Two days later, they were joined by the 291st Artillery Brigade, with its 220mm *Uragan* MLRSs and 152mm Msta-B guns. Meanwhile, long-range S-300PS SAM systems were deployed to control Crimea's airspace and Bastion-P coastal defence missile batteries were emplaced around the coast. The K-300P Bastion-P (SS-C-5 Stooge) fires a P-800 *Oniks* supersonic anti-shipping missile (with a secondary surface-to-surface role) optimized for larger, high-value targets. Given that the overwhelming majority of the Ukrainian fleet was already under blockade, and the *Hetman Sahaidachny* on its own hardly represented any kind of a serious threat, the implication was that this was both a guarantee against any Western intervention and also a symbol of Moscow's determination to hold what it had seized.

ADDITIONAL RUSSIAN FORCES DEPLOYED FOR CRIMEA OPERATION

KSSO	291st Arty Bde
Elements of the 3rd, 10th, 16th and 22nd *Spetsnaz* Bdes	727th Indep Naval Inf Bn
	382nd Indep Naval Inf Bn
25th Indep *Spetsnaz* Rgt	11th Indep Coastal Defence Rocket Arty Bde
45th Indep VDV *Spetsnaz* Rgt	u/i SAM Bde
Rgt, 31st Indep Air Assault Bde	u/i Helicopter Bde (or elements which together constituted a brigade-strength force)
Elements, 76th Air Assault Div	
18th Indep Motor Rifle Bde	

CONSOLIDATION

The consolidation of Russian control after the initial phase of the operation involved: forcing Ukrainian garrisons to defect or surrender, including naval vessels, blocked in port and often stormed by marines; holding a hurried vote on uniting with Russia; and massively reinforcing the military contingent.

On 6 March, the Supreme Council of the Autonomous Republic of Crimea decided to hold a referendum on joining Russia in just ten days' time. On 16 March, the poll was held and, after a carefully managed campaign, it unsurprisingly produced a 97 per cent vote in favour. This was, of course, neither a free nor a fair poll, with naysayers silenced and the whole process conducted under the shadow of Russian guns. The international community inevitably denounced it as meaningless, but the irony is that even had it been held wholly fairly, while the result would have been less dramatic, it would still likely have been solidly in favour.

On 20 March the State Duma, the lower chamber of the Russian legislature, adopted a law on the annexation of Crimea, which Putin signed the next day. The Ukrainian parliament, the Verkhovna Rada, adopted a counter-declaration that 'Crimea was, is, and will be part of Ukraine'. Nonetheless, despite brave words that 'the Ukrainian people will never, under any circumstances, stop fighting for the liberation of Crimea', the operation was over, with over 193 ZSU bases, facilities, ships and airfields now in Russian hands.

Moscow moved quickly to assert its control over the Crimean government. Aksyonov was allowed to keep his job, but while on 10 March he had claimed that the Supreme Council of Crimea had made him commander-in-chief of the 'Crimean armed forces' and affirmed that in the first instance he would recruit a force of 1,500 from the 'self-defence force', this was quickly overtaken by the annexation. It was striking how few of the militias the Russians wanted in their forces. The police kept their jobs (all but 88 of the 10,936 of them opted to stay), and the Berkut personnel were recruited into the OMON, Russia's equivalent. Even only just over

10 per cent of the 2,240 SBU personnel in Crimea opted to be repatriated, most joining the FSB. More than 9,000 Ukrainian soldiers and sailors were welcomed into Russian service (only between 3,990 and 4,300 chose instead to be returned to the mainland). The Ukrainian marines who defected were initially used to stand up a new 501st Independent Naval Infantry Battalion for the Black Sea Fleet, but both perceived operational needs and a desire to keep the Ukrainians diluted among Russians meant that this was later reorganized into a motor rifle battalion within the 126th Independent Coastal Defence Brigade. However, with the exception of a relative handful of veterans who decided they wanted to stay in uniform – anecdotal reports put this at no more than a couple of hundred – the local militia had always been intended to be there for political show and as cannon-fodder, and Moscow no longer had any use for them.

Most of the Ukrainian fleet was quickly blockaded by the Russians and later seized. Here, Ukrainian marines and a naval officer look out at a Russian ship closing off any exit from Sevastopol Bay on 4 March. (VIKTOR DRACHEV/AFP via Getty Images)

THE CRIMEAN OPERATION

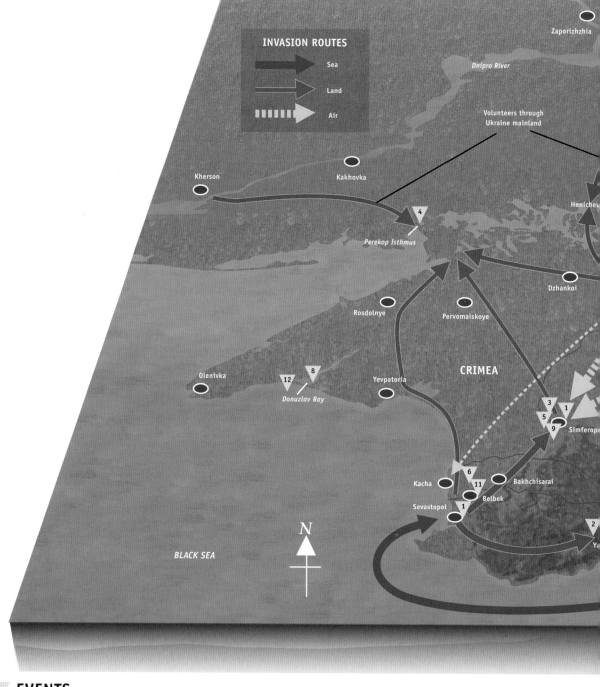

INVASION ROUTES

→ Sea

→ Land

▶ Air

Zaporizhzhia

Dnipro River

Volunteers through
Ukraine mainland

Kherson

Kakhovka

Henichev

Perekop Isthmus **4**

Dzhankoi

Rosdolnye

Pervomaiskoye

CRIMEA

Olenivka

Donuzlav Bay **12 8**

Yevpatoria

3 1
5
9 Simferop

6
Kacha **11** Bakhchisarai
Belbek
Sevastopol **1**

2

BLACK SEA

N

EVENTS

Preparation Phase

1. 23–25 February, anti-government protests
2. 25 February, Russian troops move into Yalta
3. 25 February, Russian troops secure Simferopol Airport
4. 27 February, Berkut take control of Perekop Isthmus

Invasion Phase

5. 27 February, government buildings seized
6. 27 February, Belbek airbase blockaded
7. 1 March, Kerch port taken

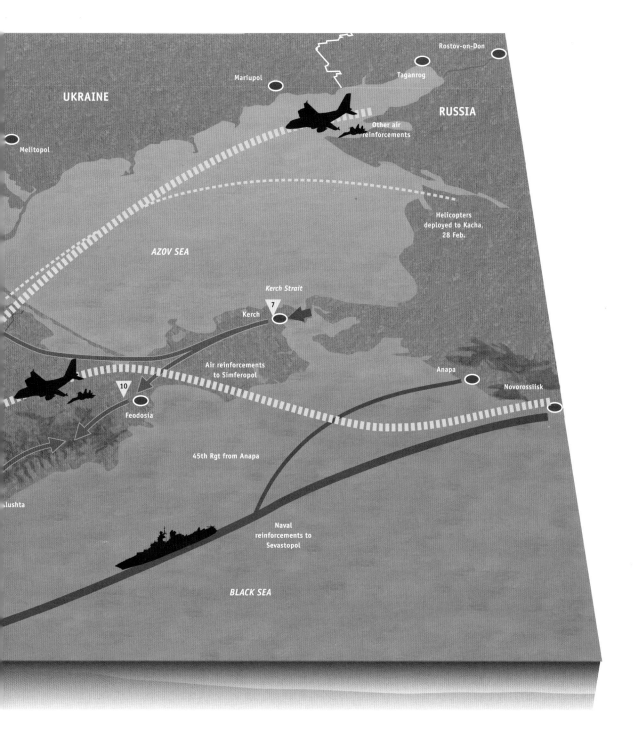

Consolidation Phase

8. 5 March, Donuzlav Bay blockaded by scuttled ships

9. 18 March, two die in storming of 13th Photogrammetric Centre

10. 21 March, KSSO storm Feodosia base

11. 22 March, Belbek taken

12. 25 March, last of 5th Surface Ship Brigade surrenders

ANALYSIS

This was at once a startling success and a Pyrrhic victory. On the one hand, it was a textbook operation that demonstrated how far Russian forces had modernized, and how they could be deployed in hybrid operations with finesse and effective coordination. On the other hand, in a way the operation proved paradoxically *too* successful, as it encouraged Moscow to try to use the same tactics in Ukraine's south-eastern Donbas region. Indeed, arguably the initial plan for the February 2022 full-scale invasion of Ukraine was to a considerable degree based on similar principles, disregarding the fact that Ukraine in 2022 was not the same as Crimea in 2014, and that whereas in the earlier operation Moscow had been able to use just the best of the best, it would be relying on much less elite forces for the later conflict.

From left to right, Chief of the General Staff General Gerasimov, Defence Minister Shoigu and President Putin, during major exercises in the Russian Far East. (ALEXEI NIKOLSKY/RIA-NOVOSTI/ AFP via Getty Images)

How special was this operation?

On one level, this was much less novel an operation than many observers at the time assumed. Expedients such as lying about one's intent, and having special forces deploy without insignia are not exactly ground-breaking.

That, for example, Putin's disavowals of the 'polite people' gave such pause says more about wishful thinking in Kyiv and many Western capitals than fiendish Russian cunning. For that matter, many of the individual aspects of the Crimean operation, from the use of local auxiliaries to efforts to encourage defections, were familiar. Even the use of cyberattacks and online disinformation to interfere with the Ukrainians' chain of command and their situational awareness used new technologies, but in the pursuit of quite traditional goals.

What was more distinctive was the scale, nature and coordination of these methods and the degree to which tactics often used only in total wars were deployed in such a small operation. It is not, for example, that other countries have not used gangsters. The Allies cut a deal with the Mafia in the Second World War to facilitate their invasion of Sicily in 1943. However, the extent to which the Kremlin was willing to enlist them as foot soldiers on the ground as well as hackers in the virtual battlefield was unexpected.

Rebels fire a salvo of BM-21 Grad rockets at Ukrainian positions outside the town of Debaltseve in February 2015. (Pierre Crom/Getty Images)

Crimea and the Donbas

The Crimean operation also had a direct impact on the subsequent Russian involvement in south-eastern Ukraine's Donbas region, although again not quite in the manner widely assumed. When Putin annexed Crimea, there was no serious thought at the time of going further: the peninsula was unique both because of its strategic value and also its historical importance. The ease with which it was taken, though, and the extent to which the Ukrainian military failed to put up a fight – or outright defected – created its own momentum and encouraged some to start thinking more ambitiously. There were those in the Donbas, a region heavily populated by Russian-speaking Ukrainians who had largely voted for Yanukovych and were uncertain about the new regime in Kyiv. They used this opportunity to mobilize but were generally not seeking to join Russia, so much as to secure for themselves more autonomy within Ukraine.

However, this created a temptation for a range of Russian nationalists, both adventurers on the ground and schemers in the Kremlin. This was particularly the case because, as Moscow consolidated its hold on Crimea, there was no more room for the badly disciplined thugs, volunteers and mercenaries of the local self-defence units. Some were recruited into the military or the police, most were disbanded – but some, unwilling to give up the adrenaline of the moment, ended up being recruited by figures such as Girkin for a new mission across the border. Initially, the Kremlin was simply willing to wait and see, to allow the activists on the ground freedom to act in this new 'grey zone' conflict. Over time, it began supplying weapons, seeing this as a potential bargaining chip with Kyiv. The shooting down in July 2014 of the civilian airliner MH17 with a Russian-supplied missile, though, forced Moscow to come off the fence. As it looked as if the government forces were going to defeat the insurgents, Putin decided to intervene directly and sent in troops to even the odds. The result would be a scrappy, miserable low-intensity conflict – that occasionally flared up into something rather more – that would last through to 2022.

Thus, victory in Crimea ended up sucking Moscow into an undeclared but politically and economically expensive war it did not want to fight for

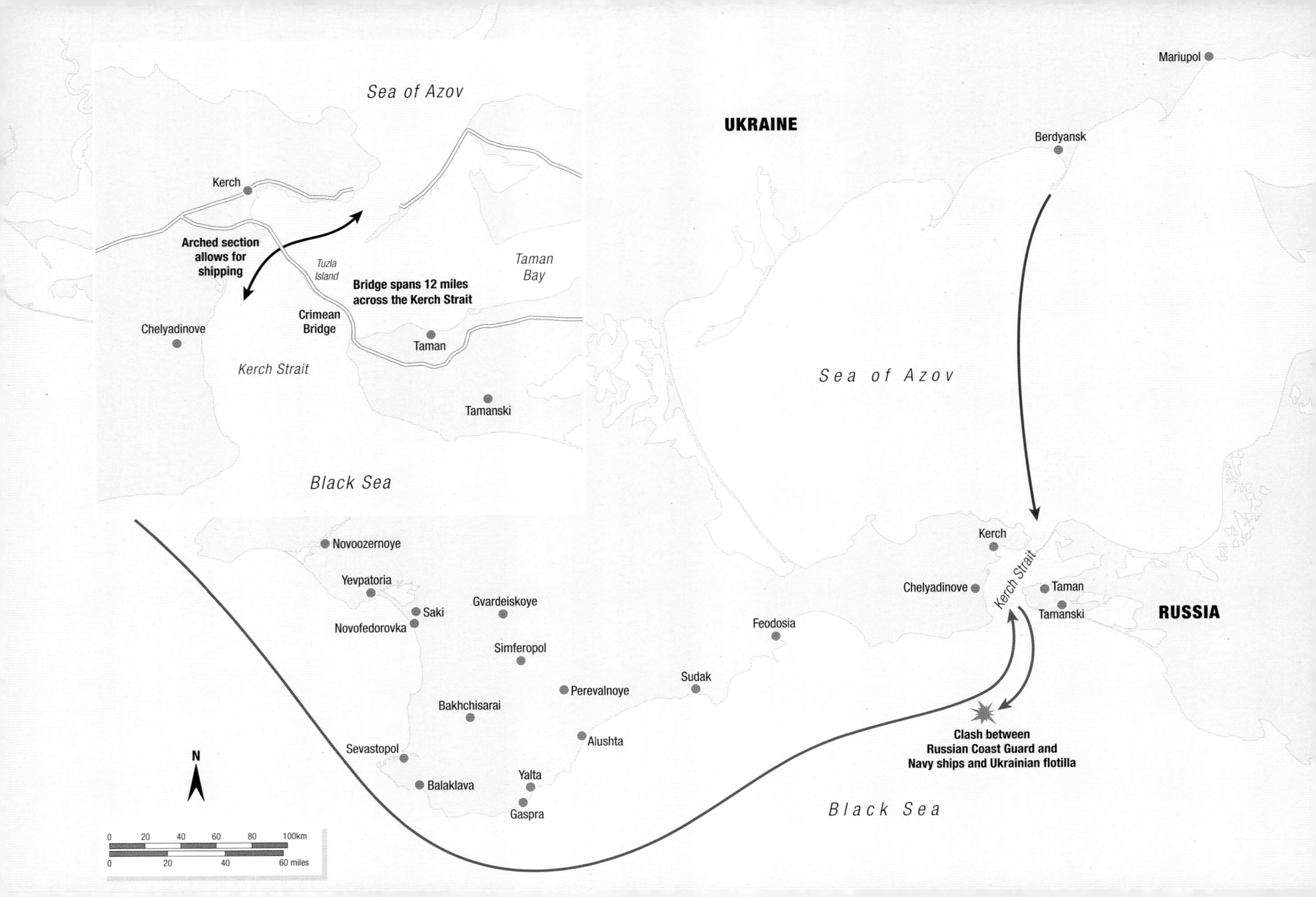

RUSSIA

UKRAINE

Maruipol

Berdyansk

Sea of Azov

Kerch

Kerch Strait

Taman

Tamanski

Chelyadinove

Clash between
Russian Coast Guard and
Navy ships and Ukrainian flotilla

Black Sea

Feodosia

Sudak

Perevalnoye

Alushta

Gvardeiskoye

Simferopol

Yalta

Gaspra

Bakhchisarai

Balaklava

Saki

Novoozernoye

Yevpatoria

Novofedorovka

Sevastopol

N

0   20   40   60   80   100km

0   20   40   60 miles

Sea of Azov

Taman
Bay

Kerch

Tuzla
Island

**Bridge spans 12 miles
across the Kerch Strait**

**Crimean
Bridge**

Taman

Tamanski

**Arched section
allows for
shipping**

Black Sea

Kerch Strait

Chelyadinove

The Kerch Strait Bridge, also known as Crimean Bridge, shortly after it was completed in 2018. (Sasha Mordovets/ Getty Images)

the Donbas, a territory it did not really want to own. Again, it used a wide range of 'grey zone' instruments, from gangsters (again, recruited to form local militias) and mercenaries, to disinformation and cyberattacks. Such situations, though, are hard to calibrate and always have serious risks of leading to more direct conflicts.

The Kerch Strait Incident

The Kerch Strait Incident of November 2018 was a measure of the way the Crimean annexation led inexorably to further conflict. The peninsula's great vulnerability was its disconnection from the Russian mainland. All supplies needed to be brought in by sea or air, and Kyiv even cut off water supplies from the North Crimean Canal. Moscow claimed – in violation of international law – the waters around Crimea and hurriedly built a 19km-(12-mile) long road and rail bridge across the Kerch Straits to the Azov Sea, connecting it to the Taman Peninsula in Russia's Krasnodar region. The bridge opened to road traffic in May 2018 and trains on December 2019.

However, the Azov Sea was no Russian lake, and two substantive Ukrainian ports – Mariupol and Berdyansk – lie on its northern shore. Under the 2003 Treaty Between the Russian Federation and Ukraine on Cooperation in the Use of the Sea of Azov and the Kerch Strait, which Putin

THE KERCH STRAIT INCIDENT, 2018

An ill-fated attempt to enter the Sea of Azov and reach Mariupol has led to a high-speed maritime chase as the Russians try to head off and seize the Ukrainian Gyurza-M-class gunboats *Berdyansk* and *Nikopol*, and their accompanying tug, the *Yany Kapu*. As the Russian FSB Coast Guard ship *Izumrud* – which is showing the damage it took when it collided with another Russian vessel earlier

in the engagement – fails to head off the *Nikopol*, it fires a burst of warning shots from its forward AK-630 gun, to no avail. It will take the Naval *Spetsnaz* embarked on the Raptor-class high-speed patrol boat P-345 *Buevlyanin* in the foreground to close before it finally surrenders. A Ka-52 attack helicopter banks overhead, not only maintaining overwatch but, as a final option, armed with B-8V20 pods, each carrying 20 80mm S-8 rockets. Higher up still is one of the pair of Su-25 attack aircraft also scrambled for this operation.

had signed, these were shared territorial waters, to which there should be no limitations on access. Ever since 2014, Moscow had been demanding that Ukrainian ships request permission to cross the strait, but with the completion of the bridge, they became increasingly aggressive in securing what they claimed were Russian waters and in inspecting – harassing – Ukrainian ships passing through.

Kyiv was not going to allow this 'sea grab' and virtual blockade of its Azov Sea ports to pass by default. On 25 November 2018, the Project 58155 Gyurza-M-class gunboats *Berdyansk* and *Nikopol*, accompanied by the tugboat *Yany Kapu*, approached the vicinity of the bridge en route to Mariupol. According to Kyiv, they had been given advance notice, but ships of the Russian Coast Guard – the maritime branch of the Border Troops, itself part of the FSB – warned them off from what they called 'Russian territorial waters'. After all, as far as the Russians were concerned, Kyiv had already challenged them when, in March, its Coast Guard in the Azov Sea had seized the Russian-flagged trawler *Nord*, even though it was operating in what Moscow considered Crimean waters.

Coast Guard vessels tried to divert the Ukrainians away, then graduated to ramming the *Yany Kapu* repeatedly. The gunboats were more agile, though, and when the Russian Coast Guard Project 22460 Okhotnik (Hunter) (NATO designation: Rubin-class) patrol boat *Izumrud* and the Project 745P Sorum-class tug *Don* tried to ram them, they actually managed instead to collide with each other. The *Izumrud* suffered visible damage from its impact with the rather larger *Don*.

When the Ukrainian flotilla refused to change course, a bulk carrier was moved to block passage under the bridge. The Ukrainians held their position some 14km (9 miles) from the bridge for eight hours, but as it became clear that the Russians were not going to open the seaway, they turned to return to Odessa.

However, the Russians had used that pause to muster their forces and also seek instructions from Moscow. Two platoons of Naval *Spetsnaz* were embarked onto rapid Project 03160 Raptor-class patrol boats, and two Su-25 jets from 37th Mixed Aviation Regiment and two Ka-52 helicopters were already in the air over the strait. As the Ukrainian flotilla turned away, a force of a dozen Russian Coast Guard and BSF vessels, including the Project 1124 Albatros-class (NATO: Grisha-class) corvette *Suzdalets*, pursued them. First the Russians fired warning shots from the 30mm AK-630M gun on *Izumrud*, then engaged them directly, while one of the Su-25s reportedly fired at least two rockets. The Ukrainian ships were boarded by the special forces and all three vessels and 24 crew detained – including some SBU officers who were present for what Kyiv would call 'routine counter-intelligence activity'.

Six of them were injured, and the *Berdyansk* was especially badly damaged, having taken hits to its bridge. The sailors would remain in Russian custody until they were part of a controversial prisoner exchange late next year, and the boats were subsequently also returned, albeit in what Kyiv claimed was a state of deliberate disrepair.

CONCLUSION

Crimea was not meant to reshape Russian operational art, for all that the West gave it disproportionate importance. However, the irony is that in many ways it also proved disastrous for the Kremlin, in that it was mistakenly adopted as a blueprint for the 2022 invasion of Ukraine.

Lessons learned – and misunderstood

Even many Russian soldiers and ex-soldiers watched the 'polite people' in Crimea with a degree of wonder and disbelief. One former paratrooper the author knew told him in May 2014 that 'this is not the army I remember from Chechnya'. An experienced Russian defence journalist was even more fulsome: 'What I see in Crimea is nothing short of the future of warfare, the future of the Russian military. Precise, disciplined, professional. I've seen our army at its worst – now I have had a chance to see it at its best.'

Of course, this was a very successful operation. The KSSO's operators had their first outing (27 February became the Day of the Special Operations Forces, in what was officially nothing to do with Crimea, but patently everything to do with it), and a combination of threat, deception, subversion and disruption, with the right mix of careful planning and field improvisation, worked beyond Moscow's expectations. The experience also allowed for some fine-tuning to the capabilities of the Defence Ministry's new National Defence Management Centre (*see* box), which was in the last stages of being commissioned.

Most Russians – including many harsh critics of his regime – were euphoric about what they regarded as a righting of a historic wrong. It is not just that Putin gained a massive popularity boost – his personal approval ratings shot up to over 80 per cent – but Defence Minister Sergei Shoigu and the whole military gained almost cult status for a while. It seemed wholly to vindicate the reforms that Shoigu and Gerasimov had implemented, and signal Russia's re-emergence as a military power able to wield not just the usual sledgehammer, but also the scalpel.

The easy victory in Crimea – and the impressive appearance of the military during carefully rehearsed exercises and parades – helped convince Putin that his armed forces were stronger than they really were. Here, T-90 tanks drive through Red Square during the 2014 Victory Day parade rehearsals. (Leonid Faerberg/SOPA Images/LightRocket via Getty Images)

What the professionals appreciated, but the politicians arguably did not, was that this was a very unusual conflict. The Ukrainian state was in virtual collapse, the Crimean population were generally supportive, or at least (apart from the Tatars) felt they had no reason to resist, Russian troops and political allies were already in place, and it was a small enough operation that it could largely be entrusted to elite forces. Besides, the Ukrainians themselves took a long time to appreciate the real nature of the threat they faced. The 36th Brigade, for example, which arguably was best placed to offer a serious response, was until relatively late apparently still convinced it was threatened not by Russian regulars but ramshackle militia and angry crowds. Instead of preparing for serious combat, it was issuing its men

THE NATIONAL DEFENCE MANAGEMENT CENTRE

Even before Crimea, the Russian military had been increasingly aware that the complex, fast-moving military-political operations of the future would demand far greater situational awareness and communications capacity than the old Central Command Post of the General Staff. As a result, in December 2013, Putin signed into existence the National Defence Management Centre (NTsUO: *Natsionalny Tsentr Upravleniya Oboronoi*), a high-tech new command post deep in the well-protected basement of the Defence Ministry building on Znamenka Street, to the west of the Kremlin. Built around what is meant to be the most powerful military supercomputer in the world, it was fully operational by late 2014, and became the hub for future regular and hybrid military operations, from the Syrian intervention to counter-insurgency operations in the Russian North Caucasus. From the Centre, commanders and planners can watch real-time feeds from drones and helmet cameras in the field, tap into the databases of 70 federal agencies, from the police to air traffic control, and maintain secure communications with the Kremlin and any of Putin's numerous palaces. However, what is meant to be an opportunity can also be a curse, and it is an open secret that some commanders in Moscow are tempted to take advantage of this to try to micro-manage operations on the ground even down to company level.

A Russian soldier stands guard in front of an S-300 long-range SAM system on Cape Fiolent. This was originally a Ukrainian S-300 but was seized by the Russians and then supplemented with their own. (VIKTOR DRACHEV/AFP via Getty Images)

improvised shields and truncheons and putting them through basic public order drills. All told, one would be hard-pressed to come up with more propitious circumstances for a land-grab.

It is not just Russia that arguably read too much into the Crimean operation, though. Having for so long become accustomed to lazy stereotypes about the 'mighty but clumsy bear', reinforced by the experiences of the Chechen and Georgian wars,[5] the sight of the 'little green men' efficiently taking over Crimea and the absence of gratuitous violence or obvious blunders led for a while to an over-correction in the West. The tactics used to take the peninsula were imagined to be 'Russia's new way of war' in the furore over the aforementioned mythical 'Gerasimov Doctrine', and the degree to which the military had been successfully reformed was dramatically over-stated. Again, the professionalism of a relative handful of elite troops was somehow taken as exemplary of the entire Russian military.

The Crimean bastion

Meanwhile, Crimea – already a relatively militarized territory – was being turned into a veritable bastion. In 2015, Putin would crow that 'we made a fortress out of Crimea. As much from the sea as from the land'. As of the start of 2021 – before the deliberate further build-up that culminated in the 2022 invasion – Russian forces on the peninsula had swollen to an estimated 31,500. The main ground forces unit is the 22nd Army Corps. This is technically part of the Black Sea Fleet, in line with a new emphasis on joint commands in which units of different arms of service will be brought together into multi-domain forces. Nonetheless, it was, before suffering

---

5   See Mark Galeotti, *Russia's Five-Day War*, Elite series (Osprey, 2023) and *Russia's Wars in Chechnya 1994–2009*, Essential Histories series (Osprey, 2014).

A Russian Sukhoi Su-24 bomber lands at the Russian base of Hmeymim. The Black Sea Fleet was from the first a crucial element in Moscow's intervention in Syria. (PAUL GYPTEAU/AFP via Getty Images)

heavy losses as a result of the invasion, a formidable force comprising the 127th Independent Reconnaissance Brigade (a relatively elite unit), the 15th Independent Coastal Rocket Artillery Brigade with K-300P Bastion-P (SS-C-5) and Bal-E (SS-C-6) missile launch complexes, the 8th Artillery Regiment, the 1096th Independent Anti-Aircraft Missile Regiment, and the marines of the 126th Independent Coastal Defence Brigade. Crimea was also still the base of the BSF's 810th Naval Infantry Brigade as well as approximately 900 Naval *Spetsnaz* in the 431st OMRPSN and paratroopers of the 7th Air Assault Division's 171st Independent Regiment. In 2015, a new unit, the 127th Independent Reconnaissance Brigade, was also stood up in Crimea, a relatively elite formation with especially extensive drone and electronic warfare capabilities, regarded in many ways as a *Spetsnaz*-equivalent force, but under direct local command (as compared with the *Spetsnaz* that are ultimately a strategic asset subordinated to the General Staff).

What was regarded – before it was tested in war with Ukraine in 2022 and found distinctly wanting – as an almost-impermeable, integrated, multi-layer air defence screen was provided by new S-400 Triumf (SA-21) long-range SAMs supplemented by medium-range Buk-M3 (SA-27) missile launchers and Pantsir-S1 (SA-22) gun/missile trucks. Nor did the peninsula's forces lack their own airpower, with the 43rd Independent Naval Aviation Regiment at Saki airbase, equipped with Su-24M bombers and Su-30SM fighters. The Air Force's 37th Mixed Aviation Regiment at Gvardeyskoye fielded a squadron of Su-24M bombers and another of Su-25SM ground attack aircraft, while the 38th Fighter Aviation Regiment at Belbek comprised a mix of Su-27 and Su-30 fighters. In addition, the 39th Helicopter Regiment at Dzhankoy had 38 gunships, a mix of Mi-28s, Mi-35s and Ka-52s.

As a result, Crimea was not only being made more defensible, but it also became a power projection hub across the Black Sea and beyond. The Black Sea Fleet, for example, would play a crucial role in Russia's intervention in Syria from 2015. Its main role was to support the rotating Permanent Naval Task Force in the Mediterranean Sea, delivering supplies and providing fire support. Periodically, the BSF flagship *Moskva* took over command duties of the Task Force, while the BSF's Project 636.3 Varshavyanka (NATO: Improved Kilo) submarines launched a number of strikes on rebel command posts and supply bases, using *Kalibr* (3M14K version, with the NATO designation SS-N-30A) supersonic cruise missiles, initially the *Rostov-on-Don*, at the time deployed into the Mediterranean. Surface ships

THE BLACK SEA FLEET, 2021

Headquarters (Sevastopol)
Flagship, Missile Cruiser *Moskva*
30th Surface Ship Div
    11th Anti-Sub Ship Bde (Sevastopol) – 5 frigates, 1 corvette
    197th Landing Ship Bde, military unit 72136 (Sevastopol) – 6 landing ships
41st Sevastopol Order of Nakhimov Rocket Boat Bde (Sevastopol)
    166th Small Missile Boat Div (Sevastopol) – 2 hovercraft attack boats
    295th Sulinsky Missile Boat Div (Sevastopol) – 4 corvettes
4th Konstanz Order of Ushakov Indep Sub Bde (Novorossiysk) – 7 diesel-electric submarines
68th Coastal Defence Ship Bde (Sevastopol)
    400th Anti-Sub Ship Div – 3 corvettes
    418th Minesweeper Bn – 4 minesweepers
184th Coastal Defence Ship Bde (Novorossiysk)
    181st Small Anti-Sub Div – 3 corvettes
    170th Minesweeper Div – 5 minesweepers
    136th Anti-Saboteur Squadron – 6 patrol boats
183rd Search & Rescue Div (Novorossiysk) – 7 various vessels
519th Indep Recon Ship Div (Sevastopol) – 4 intelligence vessels
176th Expeditionary Oceanographic Ship Div – 3 survey ships
9th Marine Support Vessel Bde (Sevastopol) – 9 various vessels
22nd Army Corps (Simferopol)
    15th Guards Coastal Missile Arty Bde (Sevastopol)
    126th Coastal Defence Bde (Perevalnoye)
    127th Indep Recon Bde (Sevastopol)
    8th Arty Rgt (Simferopol)
    854th Coastal Missile Rgt (Sevastopol)
    171st Indep Air Assault Bn (Novostepove)
    56th Guards Air Assault Rgt (Feodosia)
11th Coastal Missile Arty Bde (Utash, Krasnodar region)
Naval Infantry
810th Guards Naval Inf Bde
    880th Naval Inf Bn
    881st Naval Inf Air-Assault Bn
    888th Naval Inf Recon Bn
    1613th Arty Battery
    1619th AD Battery
382nd Naval Inf Bn
431st Naval Recon Special Designation Point
Aviation and Air Defence
2nd Guards Naval Aviation Div (Sevastopol)
    43rd Indep Naval Maritime Attack Aviation Rgt (Gvardeyskoye)
    318th Mixed Aviation Rgt (Kacha)
    37th Composite Aviation Rgt (Simferopol)
    38th Guards Fighter Aviation Rgt (Sevastopol)
39th Helicopter Rgt (Dzhankoi)
31st Air Defence Div (HQ: Sevastopol)
    12th AA Missile Rgt
    18th AA Missile Rgt
51st Air Defence Div (Rostov-on-Don)
    1537th AA Missile Rgt (Novorossiysk)
    1721st AA Missile Rgt (Sochi)
    1536th AA Missile Rgt (Rostov-on-Don)
Permanent Naval Task Force in the Mediterranean Sea – comprising rotating collection of vessels from BSF and other fleets
NB: In Russian naval (but not Naval Infantry) use, a 'division' is not, as in the army, a formation larger than a brigade, but generally used to denote a force of smaller vessels potentially operating autonomously.

of the BSF including the frigates *Admiral Grigorovich* and *Admiral Essen* also participated in these long-range attacks. Furthermore, right at the start of the intervention, a battalion from the 810th Naval Infantry Brigade was deployed to defend Russian facilities, notably the Hmeymim airbase and the Russian command post in Syria.

Crimea and the 2022 invasion

The annexation triggered a series of Western economic sanctions. This was irksome for the Kremlin, especially as it coincided with a fall in global oil prices and was combined with a series of personal sanctions that froze the assets of figures associated with the invasion and limited their travel. It was far from unbearable, though, and the Russian economy could and did adapt. However, it certainly contributed to a continued worsening of relations between Russia and the West as, in a vicious circle, each side saw itself as only responding to the other's hostile moves. It is easy to forget that Kremlin rhetoric about the CIA (and Britain's MI6) being behind the Revolution of Dignity, and the threat of NATO expansion into Ukraine, while hard to credit, reflected real fears among many of the paranoid remnants of the Soviet KGB dominating the Kremlin.

In any case, the Crimean annexation, which had been envisaged as a one-off move to take advantage of a particular opportunity and also to protect a crucial strategic asset, was to prove just the start of a new round of further worsening relations between Moscow and both Kyiv and the West. In part this was because it generated a degree of confidence in some Russian government circles that bordered on hubris. The author remembers a conversation with a thinktanker very close to the Russian Security Council apparatus, who in early 2015 flatly asserted, with apparent conviction, that 'having seen what we were able to do in Crimea, the [West] will know better than to treat Russia with its usual contempt. We demonstrated that the Russian armed forces were the best in the world, and what we did in Crimea, we can do wherever we please'.

The trouble was that such grandiose assumptions seemed quite commonplace, albeit largely not within the military itself. They were on the whole aware of the specificities of this case, and also the genuine qualitative and quantitative imbalances between Russia and NATO. They were essentially reluctantly forced into the Donbas, ordered in by a political leadership that was more interested in keeping the war going than developing any clear vision of what victory would look like. The generals were much happier with the Syrian intervention from 2015, an essentially arm's-length and small-footprint operation where Syrian troops, Lebanese militias and mercenaries such as the Wagner Group could take on the dangerous close-quarters battle while the regular Russian military essentially confined itself to intelligence and long-range fire support.

The success of the Syrian operation, though, proved another trap for the military. Shoigu – a civilian rather than a soldier, and one keen to maintain good relations with Putin – was an assiduous cheerleader for the armed forces and helped convey a sense that they were more effective, coherent and

reformed than they really were. This can often be a strategic asset, especially given that the West was to a degree also taken in by this Potemkin army. When Putin began a major build-up of forces along Ukraine's border in spring 2021, it had a sobering effect in both Kyiv and Western capitals. By the end of January 2022, this force amounted to over 100 battalion tactical groups (BTGs), equivalent to more than six times the total commitment to Crimea. Although the pretence was that these were involved in nothing more than exercises and training, their political and economic impact was considerable. Ukraine's economy took a serious hit, as investors lost their nerve under the shadow of Russian guns. Western politicians began flocking to Moscow to petition Putin to stay his hand, while some of them counselled Ukraine's President Volodymyr Zelensky to make concessions in the name of peace. Meanwhile, the Kremlin also maintained its campaigns of subversion, disinformation and occasional outright terrorism, to keep Ukraine divided and on edge.

As a gambit of 'political war', this military build-up proved inspired. Indeed, until February 2022, it is probably fair to say that Putin looked like he was winning in his long-term 'grey zone' campaign to force Ukraine to heel. Throughout this time, though, he had been havering as to whether actually to invade, and on the whole, the military high command clearly believed their role was to be no more than a muscular bluff. The problem was that the people on whom Putin increasingly had come to rely for strategic guidance were, like Security Council Secretary Nikolai Patrushev

Putin chairs a fateful meeting of his Security Council in the Kremlin on 21 February 2022, at which he made it clear that he was set on war with Ukraine. (ALEXEY NIKOLSKY/Sputnik/AFP via Getty Images)

A Russian soldier patrols in a street of conquered Mariupol in April 2022, the strategic port city that was taken after a long and devastating siege. (ALEXANDER NEMENOV/ AFP via Getty Images)

and FSB Director Alexander Bortnikov, veterans of the KGB, with no military experience. In mid-February, Putin finally decided that he would invade, after all, as taking Ukraine would be the crowning glory to his presidency. It would, he seems to have thought, elevate him to the ranks of Russia's state-builders alongside the likes of Ivan the Great (who 'gathered the Russian lands' in the 15th century), Peter the Great (who made Russia a true European power in the late 17th and early 18th centuries) and even Stalin (whose mass terror is increasingly ignored in Putin's Russia in favour of his role as architect of victory against Hitler).

In Russian military doctrine, there is a clear sense of how such a major war against a country of more than 40 million people would be fought, involving a long, careful build-up, a devastating preliminary Massed Missile-Aviation Strike (MRAU) and then a combined-arms ground offensive along a limited number of axes. The actual invasion of 24 February 2022 was very different. Most of the commanders involved had no more than a week's notice, and there were only fuel, ammunition and other consumables stocked up for two weeks of war. There was a rather limited preliminary series of air and missile attacks, but then an attempt to launch a lightning strike to take Kyiv, first with a no more than battalion-strength assault on Antonov Airport at Hostomel, just outside the capital. Meanwhile, forces crossed the border in what looked like a dozen different axes of advance, from the north towards Kyiv, out of Crimea to Kherson and along the Azov Sea coast, westwards out of Luhansk and Donbas, and across the north-eastern border.

Putin's belief seems to have been that the Ukrainian government could quickly be detained or forced to flee, with Kyiv falling in at most three days. With no leaders, the Ukrainians would largely reconcile themselves to the installation of a puppet regime, and while some isolated military units would fight, the main threat would be protests and sporadic terrorism. This would be dealt with by the National Guard security troops who also made up a substantial proportion of the invading force. Within two weeks, Ukraine would be under Moscow's control.

Except that it didn't work out like that. The ZSU, the Ukrainian armed forces, had been preparing for eight years for just such an occasion, and were also the recipients of detailed intelligence on Russian plans and capabilities from the US and UK. More to the point, the Ukrainian nation proved passionately willing to resist. At the same time, the Russian military was clearly not prepared for this war. It was still operating at peacetime manning levels, had insufficient supplies, lacked detailed operational plans, and in the main did not understand quite why it was fighting its neighbour, unconvinced by the Kremlin's rhetoric about 'Nazis in Kyiv'. Zelensky did not flee, Kyiv did not fall, the Russians were forced to focus their efforts on the Donbas and the south-east, and within three months, their casualties were equivalent to the total losses suffered by the Soviet Union in ten years of war in Afghanistan.

As of writing, in summer 2022, the war seems stalemated, although the ZSU are becoming more effective by the day thanks to both tactical

A Ukrainian soldier walks past the wreckage of Russian armour destroyed during the initial attack on Kyiv. (SERGEI SUPINSKY/AFP via Getty Images)

innovation and Western military aid. However, as the first, quiet critiques of what happened emerge from the Russian side, it seems clear that the war was driven not by the generals but by the security and intelligence community – and that the seizure of Crimea had been taken as a template for Putin's 'special military operation' (as he called it, unwilling to admit it was a full-scale war). As one former Russian officer who had been involved in the Crimean operation put it to the author:

> It was insane... They seem to have believed that what could be done in a friendly peninsula when the [government] was in chaos could just be scaled up to the whole damn country. That ordinary motor-riflemen could be as disciplined and competent as [Naval Infantry] and *Spetsnaz*, that the Ukrainians would welcome us with bread and salt and folk dancing, and that the West would sit back and let us roll up to NATO's borders. They really did think that this was going to be Crimea all over again, and didn't bother asking us, the professionals, first. And so, they completely f***ed us all.

This is not the first time the Kremlin has made disastrous misjudgements about wars based on a misunderstanding of past experiences and a reluctance to consult its own generals. When he invaded Afghanistan in 1979, Soviet leader Leonid Brezhnev appears to have assumed it would be a largely bloodless and brief exercise in intimidation, like the 1968 invasion of Czechoslovakia, and while his Chief of the General Staff Marshal Nikolai Ogarkov was dead set against the operation, fully aware of just how inaccurate the parallel was, his advice was never sought. Likewise, there seems little evidence that this time Putin looked for the advice of his generals or that Shoigu was willing to force him to listen. Instead, the intelligence officers based their 'special military operation' on a flawed and dangerous parallel. Perhaps the tragic irony of the Crimean annexation is that by its very success it seduced the Kremlin into a dangerously exaggerated notion of its capabilities – and paved the way for a bloody war that it is likely not able to win.

FURTHER READING

Arutunyan, Anna. *Hybrid Warriors: Proxies, Freelancers and Moscow's Struggle for Ukraine* (Hurst, 2022)

DeBenedictis, Kent. *Russian 'Hybrid Warfare' and the Annexation of Crimea: The Modern Application of Soviet Political Warfare* (Bloomsbury, 2022)

Galeotti, Mark. *Russian Political War. Moving Beyond the Hybrid* (Routledge, 2019)

Galeotti, Mark. *The Weaponisation of Everything* (Yale University Press, 2022)

Howard, Colby & Ruslan Pukhov (eds). *Brothers Armed. Military Aspects of the Crisis in Ukraine*, 2nd edition (EastView, 2015)

Johnsson, Oscar and Robert Seely. 'Russian Full-Spectrum Conflict: An Appraisal After Ukraine', *Journal of Slavic Military Studies*, 28, No. 1 (2015): 1–22

Maigre, Merle. 'Nothing New in Hybrid Warfare: The Estonian Experience and Recommendations for NATO', *German Marshall Fund of the United States Policy Brief*, February 2015

Melvin, Mungo. *Sevastopol's Wars: Crimea from Potemkin to Putin* (Osprey, 2017)

Messner, Evgeny. *Myatezh: imya tretyey vsemirnoy* (Chtets, 2018)

Rácz, András. *Russia's Hybrid War in Ukraine* (Finnish Institute of International Affairs, 2015)

Savinkin, A. E. and I. V. Domnin (eds). *Groznoe oruzhie: Malaia voina, partizanstvo i drugie vidy asimmetrichnogo voevaniya v svete naslediya russkikh voennykh myslitelei* (Russkii put', 2007)

INDEX

References to images are in **bold**.

Abisov, Sergei 45
afgantsy (Afghanistan veterans) 29
Afghanistan 11–13, 77–78
   aircraft, Russian 72
   Il-76: **34**, 35
Aksyonov, Sergei 30–31, 37, 44–45, 58
Andryushyn, Col Andriy 49–50
Arab Spring 14
Arabat Arrow 56–57
Avakov, Arsen 30
Avrutsky, Igor 45
Azov Sea 65, 68

Balaklava 41
Baskaki gang 32, 35, 42
Belaventsev, Oleg 31–32, 35
Berezovsky, Rear Adm Denis 45–47
Berkut riot police 10, 17, **18–19**, 29, 58
   and checkpoints 37–38
Bērziņš, Jānis 20
Black Sea Fleet (BSF) **6**, 7–8, **21**, 37, 71–74
   and preparations 23, 25, **26**, 33–34
   and Ukrainian Navy 47–48
   blockades 48–49, 51–53
Bochkala, Roman 42
Bolshevik Revolution 6, 12, 29–30
Borodai, Alexander 32
Bortnikov, Alexander 23, 76
Brezhnev, Leonid 78

Central Military District 33
Chaly, Aleksey 17, 28–30
Chechnya 11, 71
'Colour Revolutions' 14
Communists 12
Cossacks 11, **12**, 28, 29, 39
   and bases 50–51
   and Kuban Army 40
   and navy 45–46
Crimean bastion 71–73
Crimean operation **60–61**, 62–63
Crimean War (1854–55) 5–6
cyberattacks 4, 17, 20
Czechoslovakia 78

Delyatitsky, Lt Col Dmitry 53
disinformation 11
Donbas 4, 9, 16, 63, 65

Estonia 12, 20
Euromaidan 8–10, 27
European Union (EU) 9

Fedash, Capt Yuri 47
Fedun, Capt Valentin 49–50
Feodosia 40, 45, 48, 51, 53
'For the Return of Crimea' medal 22–23
FSB (Federal Security Service) 17, 23, 32, 59

gangsters 4, 16, 20, 32, 34–35, 63
Georgia 11, 14, 20, 71
Georgy Pobedonosets (ship) 39
Gerasimov, Gen Valery 14–16, **62**, 69, 71
Girkin, Igor ('Strelkov') 32, 36–37, 49–50, 63
Great Britain 5, 77
grey zone warfare 4, 20
GRU (military intelligence) 17, 20, 23, 49

Hayduk, Rear Adm Serhiy 46, 51–52
Hetman Sahaidachny (ship) 43
Hezbollah 20
hybrid warfare 4, 20

Ilyin, Adm Yuri 31
Ivanov, Sergei 23
Ivanovets (ship) 41, **42**

Kaliningrad (ship) 39
Karachevsky, Maj Stanislav 50
Kazakov, Ruslan 49–50
Kennan, George 13–14
Kerch ferry 39–40
Kerch Strait Incident (2018) 65, **66–67**, 68
KGB 10, 14, 23, 74
Kievan Rus' 5
Klintsevich, Frants 29
Kokurin, ENS Serhiy 49
Konstantinov, Vladimir 34
Kozhyn, Adm Borys 7
Kravchuk, Leonid 7
KSSO *see* Special Operations Forces Command (KSSO)

Lavrov, Sergei 23
Lenin, Vladimir 29–30
local militias 29, 35, **36**, 49

Main Operations Directorate (GOU) 21–23
Malofeyev, Konstantin 32
Mamchur, Col Yuly 38–39, 44, 53
Marchenko, Maj Dmytro 56
media 41–42
Melnichenko, Viktor 45
mercenaries 16–17
Messner, Yevgeny 13
MH17 airliner 63
Minsk (ship) 39
Mogilev, Anatoly 36–37
Mohyliov, Anatoly 27
Mongols 5
Mosiychuk, Igor 30
MVS (Ukrainian Ministry of Internal Affairs) 10, 25, 30, 36, 56

Nalyvaichenko, Valentyn 42
National Defence Management Centre (NTsUO) 69–70
NATO 74
Night Wolves **15**, 16–17, 28
Novofedorovka 41, 50–51

Ogarkov, Gen Nikolai 78
Olenegorsky Gornyak (ship) 39

paramilitaries 25–26
Patrushev, Nikolai 23, 75–76
people's militia **13**
'people's squads' *see* local militias
Perekop Isthmus 17, **18–19**, 40, 56
Pereyaslav Agreement (1654) 6
Peter the Great 76
police **30**, 31, 36, 45, 48, 58
political warfare 13–14
Poroshenko, Petro 9, 42
preparations 23, 25–26, 33–35
Putin, Vladimir 8–10, 13, **62**, 69
   and armed forces 44
   and consolidation 58
   and Crimea 22–23, 71
   and Donbas 63
   and Girkin 32
   and Kerch Strait 65, 68
   and Night Wolves 16
   and Ukraine 75–78
   and zero hour 27, 35

Ratnik personal equipment suite 35–36
Roman Empire 4–5
Rubezh (Borderline) militia 37
Russia 7–9, 13–16, 58–59, 69–70

Russian Army 33, 35–36, 74–75
   22nd Army Corps 71–72
   45th VDV Rgt 21
Russian Civil War (1918–22) 6, 11–12
Russian Empire 5–6
Russian language 27
Russian Unity party 29–30

Saki airbase 41, 51
Salem gang 32, 34–35, 42
SBU (Security Service of Ukraine) 28, 30, 40–41, 59
Sea Guard 41, 46
Second World War (1939–45) 6
Sevastopol 5, 6, 8, 17, 28–29, 44–45
Shakuro, Rear Adm Dmitry 48
Shoigu, Sergei 23, 31, **62**, 69, 74–75, 78
Simferopol **27**, 34, 38, 40, 45
   and 13th Photogrammetric Centre 49–50
Slavutych (ship) 47–48
Slutsky, Leonid 31
Solntsevo group 32
Soviet Union 6–7, 11–13
Special Operations Forces Command (KSSO) 33–34, 36, 53, **54–55**, 69
Stalin, Joseph 6, 29, 76
subversion 4, 11, 13–14
Svoboda (Freedom) movement 30
SVR (Foreign Intelligence Service) 17
Syria 16, 73–74

Tatars 5–6, 29–30, 34–35
Tauric Peninsula 4–5
telecommunications 41–42
Tenyukh, Adm Ihor 31, 42
titushki (thugs) 9
Tolmachev, Capt Alexander 41
Transnistria **22**
Tyagnibok, Oleg 30

Ukraine 6–8, 20, 27–31, 58–59
   and 2022 invasion 4, 16, 75–78
   and bases 50–53
   and Berkut riot police 17
   and border guards **22**
   and Euromaidan 8–10
   and Kerch Strait 65, 68
   and Mamchur 38–39
   and Orange Revolution 14
   see also Donbas
Ukrainian Army 25, 28, 42–44, 77–78
   36th Bde 70–71
Ukrainian Navy 45–48
United States of America (USA) 14, 77
Units of Special Designation 11

Vladimir of Kiev, Prince 5
Voronchenko, Maj Gen Igor 53

Wagner Group Private Military Company 16, 74
warfare 11–16
West, the 14–16, 71, 74–75, 78
Wrangel, Gen Pyotr 6

Yanukovych, Viktor 9–10, 17, 21
Yatsenyuk, Arseny 9, 51
Yatsuba, Vladimir 30
Yeliseyev, Vice Adm Sergei 45
Yeltsin, Boris 7
Yukalo, Alexander 49–50
Yushchenko, Viktor 8

Zaitsev, Sgt Yevgeny 50
Zaldostanov, Alexander 'Surgeon' **15**, 16, 44
Zelensky, Volodymyr 75, 77
zero hour (*Vremya Cha*) 27, 35–37
Zima, Pyotr 28, 45